Stricken:

The 5,000 Stages of Grief

Stricken:

The 5,000 Stages of Grief

edited by

Spike Gillespie

and Katherine Tanney

Dalton Publishing

AUSTIN, TEXAS

Dalton Publishing
P.O. Box 242
Austin, Texas 78767
www.daltonpublishing.com

Printed in the United States of America

Edited by Spike Gillespie and Katherine Tanney

Assisted editing by Ric Williams and Neil Kahn

Cover photography by Mary Stephens

Cover design by Tamar Design+Marketing

Interior design and typesetting by Deltina Hay

ISBN-13: 978-0-9817443-6-0

Library of Congress Cataloging-in-Publication Data

Stricken-- the 5,000 stages of grief / edited by Spike Gillespie and Katherine Tanney.
p. cm.
ISBN 978-0-9817443-6-0
1. Grief. 2. Loss (Psychology) I. Gillespie, Spike. II. Tanney, Katherine. III. Title: Stricken-- the five thousand stages of grief. IV. Title: 5,000 stages of grief.
BF575.G7S767 2009
155.9'3--dc22

2008044791

This book is dedicated to Sandy Silver,

and to the memory of her son, Christopher Kern

xxx, ooo

Spike Gillespie

Editor's Note

ON JANUARY 31, 2007, Molly Ivins died. Molly was my great friend and long time mentor. She wasn't your typical mentor. She gave me advice like, "If you're a starving writer, save your pennies and feed your cat, because you can trick your hungry stomach into feeling full with a glass of water, but you cannot shut up a hungry cat."

Molly was the busiest person I knew, and yet she always made time to take me to lunch, tell me her wild stories, and encourage me in all of my writerly dreams. She also loved my son, whom she first met when he was around seven. Long after Henry stopped hanging out with me, the one party he always still wanted to join me at was Final Friday, monthly bashes where Molly threw open her doors and all manner of hilarity and political satire ensued. I swear we must've gone to at least 80 of those events over the years.

When Molly's cancer came back for the ninetieth time, I got really nervous when my cell phone indicated an incoming call from Betsy, her assistant. This nervousness gave way to deep sadness when I got the call I was dreading: Molly was at the end.

I had the honor and privilege of spending a number of Molly's final days at her bedside, holding her hand, telling her I loved her, kissing her fuzzy bald head goodbye. My son, too, had his chance for a farewell, and I could see something had changed permanently in him when we got back on the hospital elevator, after he saw her that one last time.

Sarah Barnes, who used to share those lunches with Molly and me, called me around six p.m. that Wednesday night to ask if I'd heard the news. I had not. I curled up in a ball and cried.

The next night, my then husband announced I had two choices. I could either cease all contact with him for a period of time—some months—a period he would determine without my input, at which point he would consider trying to work on our disaster of a marriage. Or I could have a flat out divorce.

I don't suppose it's ever "good timing" to walk out on one's spouse. But I found his timing to be especially harsh. The double whammy of losing my friend and my marriage in twenty-four hours leveled me. Totally.

Over the next several months, I fell apart. I came very close, quite literally, to having a nervous breakdown. I could not force food into my body. I chain-smoked. I lost forty pounds in about ten minutes. And I cried every single day. For six months. I was astounded at my body's ability to produce so many tears.

Back in 1986, I had a miscarriage. I locked myself in my room and decided I would never come out again. My mother explained to me this was not going to be the case. I was, she informed me, going to get my ass out of bed, get dressed, and go to work. And so, begrudgingly, I did, surprised at the comfort this distraction brought me.

My mother's advice came back to me in 2007 and, though large stores of my memory from the first half of that year escape me, I do know this: I was busy. I was really, really busy and purposefully so. I embraced this busyness because, though it exhausted me, I knew that if I gave in fully to my grief, I was going to totally lose my shit. I recognized the value of some denial and so I buried myself in projects and travel.

Of the latter, I was fortunate enough to have many generous friends who sent me on numerous trips, which, while in the moment didn't always feel healing, in retrospect helped tremendously. I spent a week in Japan, face buried in my futon, my shoulders shaking as I sobbed. I spent another week in Ontario, at a theater festival, seeing amazing parallels between my life and countless tragic characters conjured by Shakespeare and Albee and Steinbeck.

As for burying myself in projects—this book is a direct result of that strategy. Not only did I want to process my own grief, not only did I want to work and work and work, but I also suddenly had this keen awareness of what grief felt like as I was feeling it. I wanted to give voice and shape to that. So I called upon my friends to offer their stories of grief.

In the request I sent out for essays, I made it clear that I was not looking for neat and tidy pieces that echoed some sort of *Chicken Soup For The Sad Soul* pep talk. Grief does not, in my experience, respond to pep talks. Yes, being loved and supported and listened to and force fed helps. And I am so grateful to everyone who did those things for me. But in the end, the process is what it is, it winds down weird paths, and when you start to feel better, there's no sense in relaxing into it, because you never know when some little something is going to retrigger the avalanche. (Months after my ex-husband walked out on me, I ran into Whole Foods to grab something. I was instantly paralyzed—I'd bought so many meals for us there and now revisiting this place brought on a visceral reaction so great it threatened to knock me down again.)

My therapist, to whom I am forever indebted, told me that grief is like a spiral staircase. There are days when you are far from the wall of the pain and you feel like you're moving up. But then, when you least expect it, there you are, shoulder back up against the very feelings you thought were behind you.

Another good friend passed along some advice his mother gave him: *Grief takes four seasons to move through.* Which isn't to say that there is a set ending point, of course. I've had things I've grieved for decades. But I think the advice means that if you can get through that first year, life becomes more bearable. Certainly this was the case with me.

At the risk of sounding like the sort of *Chicken Soup* spoon-feeder I claimed not to be interested in hearing from, I have to say that the rough changes grief rudely foisted upon me led me to a place far better than I could imagine. Several of my phobias fell completely by the wayside. A number of my projects bore surprising fruit. And now, as I write this, I'm closing in on a year since my double loss, and I can't remember the last time I cried. But I can certainly recall the last time I ate.

This book is filled with the personal stories of people looking at grief from all sorts of angles. The title comes from an observation made by my Buddhist friend, Carlene, who pointed out that *stricken* is about as precise a description as you can get on the topic, and from Laura House, whose essay opens this collection, and who notes so well how countless the stages are.

At the end of this book are words of wisdom on how to help others in grief. These thoughts are from my friend Sandy Silver, who, in acting on her grief, gave a tremendous gift to the entire city of Austin. It was through this gift that I met her. If you've ever walked around Town Lake and seen the beautiful pink granite bench that is inscribed: XXX,OOO, Chris, you have experienced this gift.

Chris is Sandy's son, who died in 1991. Long before I ever met Sandy, I passed that bench every day, probably for ten years, as I took my daily four-mile walks. I could not put my finger on it, but that bench spoke to me. I always had the feeling that I knew Chris, though we'd never met. I mentioned this in an essay in *The Austin Chronicle*, and Sandy called me. Not long after, I was walking by one day and there she was, at the bench. We've been friends ever since. Every year, on Chris's birthday and death anniversary, I take flowers to the bench. I'm not the only one. And if you go to see it, be sure to take a look at the back, and underneath, where you'll find little treasures embedded in the granite and limestone, mementos of a beloved son.

The list of people to whom I am forever grateful for helping me in my grief is entirely too long to publish here. My inner sanctum, my son's father, my ex-brother-in-law, my therapist, the people who gave me work even when I was hardly at the top of my game, the amazing writers who joined forces with me one night to perform a spoken word production to help me heal—a production that has grown into an ongoing theatrical show.

I want to give a very special shout out to Ori, who showed up and surprised me and invited me into his world with laughter and compassion and a gentle infinite patience, particularly those many moments when I found myself on that spiral staircase, up against the wall unexpectedly, nearly too terrified to move ahead.

Another special thanks goes to Deltina for her faith in the project. There were long lags in the process because when I was deep in grief, writing about it, and reading about it was too much. And then those other times, when grief backed off and gave me a little breathing room, I found the prospect of writing and reading about the topic wholly unpalatable.

Toward that end, I have tremendous gratitude for Katherine Tanney, who agreed to tag team and co-edit this book with me. Katherine nudged me toward deadlines, brought many wonderful writers to the project, and pulled more than her share during the editing process.

—Spike Gillespie

Katherine Tanney

Editor's Note

WHEN SPIKE GILLESPIE TOLD me she was going to collect essays for a book about grief, I was in the thick of my own research on the topic. I was reading C.S. Lewis's diary following the death of his wife ("A Grief Observed") and a series of letters by Genevieve Jurgensen about the loss of her two young daughters in an auto accident ("The Disappearance"). Around this same time I became aware of Austin's Dalton Publishing when I wrote about a publication party for one of their authors in my newspaper column.

I asked Spike if I could contribute an essay and to my surprise she invited me to help her edit the project. We contacted writers and the essays began to come in. What struck me when I printed out everything and began reading the pieces as a body of interconnected parts was how isolating grief is. It's so easy to feel alone with it, stricken, as you go through your day, assuming others are happy, spared.

Weird, how grief weighs like a physical burden on you. You have to drag the sadness and anxiety and depression around with you. Your life is just as it was—same busy schedule, same good friends, sweet dogs, love of yoga, but all the joy has gone out of it. You go through the motions with the friends considerate enough to extend invitations. You dress up, show up, bathed and smelling good, as if all is just dandy. But inside the pain is sharp and will not be put off.

I wrote those words during a bout of intense grief last year, over the sudden loss—something like a miscarriage, I imagine—of a very promising young relationship.

It's my hope that the amazing variety of voices in this collection and the kinds of grief considered will offer companionship and support to those who have found themselves, or may still be, crushed in the fists of the beast.

Thanks to the gifted writers who responded to my invitation to contribute, and to Spike Gillespie and Deltina Hay at Dalton Publishing for giving me the opportunity to participate in such a worthwhile project.

—Katherine Tanney

Table of Contents

clouds form & unform

he sleeps in a narrow bed
& cannot remember his dreams

or how in heaven there are no churches
there are he imagines long beaches white &
trackless & in the distance great whales breaching

he laughs: there are ice cream trucks in heaven
& horses that smoke fine Cuban cigars
but there are no churches
& no one dreams of

being someone else or what might have
been or what will happen if there is
no heaven or hell or time enough
to say goodbye or wander
into a room of ghosts

no dreamcatchers
prayer sticks
talismans
shawls
bells
dust

how what
he cannot hold
becomes everything
worth holding
the long light
a body of
soft rain

Laura House

The Thing Bout Losing My Mom…

WE ALL KNOW THERE are stages of grief. Denial. Crying. Eating. Anger. Rage. Freak out. Bargaining. Drinking. Begging. Pleading. Sex with strangers. Reluctant acceptance. Acceptance. But these don't tell you the whole story. You actually have to go through an entire reprogramming of your brain. I mean, I had a mother every day all day long for thirty-five years. Suddenly, I didn't. Logically, I understood. She had cancer; she got sick. She's gone. Got it. But now, she's just gone? How is that possible? How is my mother never to return?

Mom got diagnosed in 2000. She called me from Texas at my new job in San Francisco. She'd never called me at work, ever. She said, "Well, I have cancer." Like that. Who does that? She just didn't see the point of beating around the bush. I was thinking plane ticket. I asked if she was going to have an operation, chemo; what was going to happen? She said that she and Dad were going to have a bowl of soup, then head to the hospital.

Record scratch. What?

"You're calling me on the way to the hospital?"

"No, I said we were going to have a bowl of soup!"

And that's my mom. Don't bother Laura with my cancer. Years before, she'd had a complication from anesthesia on an out-patient eye tuck procedure and got a blood clot on her brain.

No one in the family even called me. I was three hours away in Austin. Finally, her best friend called, "Laura, I don't know if your dad told you, but your mom has a blood clot on her brain. It's fine. Don't worry yourself, just wanted you to know."

It's fine? Is that a Texas thing? Of course I worried myself. Of course I hopped in the car and went to see her. She was a big reader and my dad and brother had gotten her some books. SHE HAD A BLOOD CLOT ON HER BRAIN. I got her books on tape.

But this was worse. This was cancer. Her mom died from it. Everybody seems to die from it. I didn't want her to die from it. But she was going to die from it.

She had three rounds of chemo over five years. The first one made her feel sick and lose her hair, but when she came out of it she joined Jenny Craig and lost seventy pounds. After the second round a year and a half later, she joined Curves. She wanted to live, and live well.

She did what she could to be healthy and kept enjoying her friends and her life. I mentioned her being sick to a friend who asked me what kind of cancer it was. I didn't know. I asked my mom. She said, "Oh, who knows?" It was ovarian. I cautiously mentioned support groups to my mom. She said, "This cancer has taken enough of my life. I'm not going to give it any more time by sitting around talking about it. I do what the doctors tell me and forget about it."

In 2005 she was having her last session in her third round of chemo. She came home and couldn't breathe. Her lungs were filling with fluid. She was too tired to walk across the room. This was the woman who, when I called months before and asked what she was up to that day, said, "Oh, going to Curves, then chemo, then the grocery store to get some potatoes to go with the chicken." Now she couldn't walk across a room. I was miles away in L.A. at the time. Dad called. Dad had never called me, ever. He said mom was sick, back in the hospital, in ICU, and he was just letting me know. Oh. I asked if I needed to come home. He said to wait till morning; maybe it'd take a turn. It did.

She wasn't dying; she'd contracted congestive heart failure from the chemo. Apparently, it's common and you can live with it, like diabetes. You stop eating salt and a few other things and you're fine.

A week and a half later, Dad called me for the second time in my life. Mom was in the hospital again. Should I come home? Again, I got the wait till morning thing. But something wasn't right.

I experienced that a lot around my mother's death. You know things. Maybe when you're close with someone who's about to enter the spirit realm, you somehow get more connected to the spirit realm. I don't know, but I do know that I knew.

I called my best friend. Her mom and my mom are best friends. I asked what the deal was. She said it was bad. Fuck it. I called her mom, Verna, the same one who'd told me about my mom's brain blood clot. I'd never called her, ever. She said it was bad. "Laura, that little light in her eyes is gone." Oh, god. Has a sadder sentence ever been said?

I called the airline to see what to do if I needed an emergency ticket the next day. I cried. I slept. When I woke up, I had a message, "Come home." I ran to work, grabbed my laptop, and hopped on a plane, bracing myself for a bad weekend. We'd get Mom home and it'd be a drag, but it'd be all right. Right?

Three things. I don't know how to say this, because I haven't experienced such a thing before or since, but when I was at the airport, about to board the plane, I felt my mom. I was wearing a denim shirt similar to one I'd gotten her. First I felt her in my shirt, and then I felt she was around me, kind of up in the air. And I felt her saying she needed to go. And I felt myself thinking to her that she should go, if she needs to. And I wouldn't argue it with a skeptic, but that's what I felt—as if my mom had astral projected to me to make sure I was okay.

Second thing. I fell asleep on the plane and dreamt my mom was dead.

Third thing. I talked to the woman next to me. Her grandmother had had congestive heart failure and she told me all about it. She was very sweet and comforting. As we were about to unload off the plane, she touched my arm. "What's your mom's name?" "Carole," I said. And then, in a voice that sounded somewhat otherworldly, she said, "Carole's gonna be fine." And not for a second did I take that to mean alive-fine. I don't know how else to explain it. It felt to me like an angel or spirit was speaking through this woman saying Mom will be fine, like, in the ultimate sense.

Another best friend of Mom's, Norma, the former school nurse who lived down the street and who took her to every chemo, picked me up. We were driving to the hospital, making chitchat as best we could, when she got a call. Her end was something like, "I've got Laura and we're on our way. Oh. Okay, well, we'll see you in a minute."

And I knew. I didn't ask. She didn't tell. But I knew that was the death call. And this wasn't in any preternatural way; this was just common sense. You could hear it in her voice. We got to the hospital, and Norma turned around with tears in her eyes and said, "She's gone. I'm so sorry."

It wasn't congestive heart failure after all. She'd gotten a viral infection that attacks the heart, looks like CHF, but takes you out very quickly.

I went upstairs in a daze and found my Dad. He and my brother walked me into a room where my mom had just died about ten minutes before. Just about as I was landing. As if she waited till I landed safely, but didn't want me to actually see her die. And I don't know that you get choices like that, but I believe if she'd had a choice, that would have been it.

Dad and I went home. A message on the phone said Mom's wine was ready to be picked up. That's so my mom, having a special order of wine, even when she was dead. I grabbed her phone book and started calling. Mom had a lot of friends. Friends from childhood, college, teaching, church. And that's when the grieving process began for me. I told people over and over for hours that my mom was dead. I just kept saying it and how it happened. I wouldn't wish that task on anyone, but I don't know how else I could have processed it.

My mom was dead and dealing with that became a near full-time job for me. Grief is serious. A friend lost both of her parents within a year and didn't grieve, and then got hit with viral meningitis, she claims, from keeping it all inside. I remembered, "Feel your feelings." And I did. When I felt a cry come on, I let it happen. Driving, eating, in line at Target—wherever. My brain had to get that she was gone. Gone gone.

My brain understood Mom being at the store, so that's what it felt like for a while. Yes, we're getting rid of her clothes and clearing out her stuff, but she's at the store. She's with a friend. She's at church. She's down the hall in the restroom. My mind kept imagining she was just elsewhere. That's all my mind could do. I had to ease into the "gone" part, I guess.

What surprised me most about grief was the surprise. I was constantly surprised that my mom was dead. It was consistently news to me. Logically, I knew. But it took time to really, really know. For a while, I'd wake up crying. I'd wake up like any other time, then it'd hit me, "Oh, another day—My mom's dead—What?—Yes, dead!—Oh, god," and cry. Or I'd be at Target. I'd see a necklace, "Mom would really like that—But she's dead—She's what?—Dead!—Oh, god!" And I'd be off again. That's why the first year is the hardest; it's three hundred sixty-five new days that you've never had without your loved one. Your birthday, their birthday, Christmas, Valentine's. Or what I found the hardest: just days. Just a Saturday and you're driving and you want to call. Just to say hi. And you can't. You can't call just to say hi. And it seeps in more and more. So very, awfully, slowly. Just that. You can never again just call to say hi to your mom.

And I know, you can pray or talk to the sky, write a letter and never send it, but fuck that. That's the hardest part for me. Not the big stuff. At Christmas, it kind of just feels like Mom is in another room in a way. Birthdays were often forgotten anyway, that's not too big a deal. But the little things. I do see necklaces she'd like and have to remind myself that she's gone. Still. Gone today and gone tomorrow.

That's the pain of grief: reminders. It's confusing. It's stark new information. It's unwanted. But it has to sink in: My mom was alive and now she's dead. And when it does, that's acceptance.

It's been two years now, almost exactly. I kept a journal of the first year. It helped to write it out. There's a lot of swearing.

There are things people don't tell you about grief. The only sense I had about it was, "I guess you're sad and cry a lot." Some people have goodbye dreams where they get to have those last words with a loved one. Or they feel their loved one in the room with them from time to time. I never had that. Know what I did get? Effing Hall and Oates "She's Gone" stuck in my head.

Like I needed that on top of everything else. Wasn't I suffering enough? I'd explain to my brain the song isn't even about dying, it's about a break-up, but she just wasn't having it. I'd innocently think, "She's gone," and we were off.

Maybe grief is new to you. If so, I'm glad it's not commonplace for you. Secondly, here's some advice.

First. Feel your feelings. Seriously. So simple, but not always easy. Sometimes instinct says to ignore our feelings. Don't. I never denied my grief. I cried through every "my mom is dead" call. It took to about Person Number 77 before I could say it without breaking down. I cried at the shoe store buying shoes for her funeral. I cried in Kohl's. I cried in the car. I pulled over if I had to. And with each bout of crying, I learned it passes. It doesn't feel like it ever will. Don't think your grief is worse than someone else's. It's grief. It's a gut-wrenching, psyche-changing process. Honor it. Pay attention. It's convulsing, painful tears. It'll go for hours. And, eventually, it'd be just an hour, then less than that. Then just once a day, then not every day. I still cry when I talk about it and I cried as I wrote most of this. I'm actually sitting in my mom's chair right now in Grand Prairie.

I cry. And if you need to cry, I can't express to you strongly enough to do it. Let it out. Better out than in, as they say.

Second. And this is maybe less clear, but powerful. You have a window of about a year. A few weeks into my grieving process, an older friend pulled me aside. He could tell I was hurting a great deal and he'd lost his mother years before. He said, "I don't know if this will make sense to you, but you have a window of about a year. After that, things pretty much go back to normal. But you have this special year. Use it. I don't know what it is for you, but for me, I wrote my book. I just want you to know you have this special year to use."

And I didn't exactly understand at the time, but kind of I did. I felt different. I felt changed. I felt closer to…Being? More fearless? The worst thing that could happen to me did, so what was I static in other areas for? What could scare me now? It was unbelievable to me that anything would ever go back to normal again, but it does. Once again, you get annoyed by traffic or you count calories or you fret about something stupid at work. All the things that were so small in light of my loss, things that I didn't even notice for a while, that I couldn't believe anyone cared about, they all come back. For a while, all I could do was be in the grief. But it lifts. I have days where I don't think about it at all. And I have days where I see a seventy-year-old at the grocery store and I start to cry. It's like that. Grief is more like the flu than anything else. It just comes on. And it passes. I used my year. I was in touch with myself. I felt very deeply. I traveled and took classes. I made huge moves on my career I'd been too timid to try before. I got my dream job and a much needed divorce. Not that you have to do any of that, specifically, but it worked for me.

Losing gives us much needed perspective. I believe that if we don't use it, we will lose it. Losing my mom was nightmarish. But it also brought the rest of my family closer. It triggered changes in me, changes I'm so grateful for. It softened my heart. It opened my eyes. It elevated my soul. I wish she were here for me to tell these things to, but that's not how it works. Grieving loss is a fundamentally necessary process. I'm so sorry you have to go through it. But I know you'll get through it. And I know you can come out better for it on the other side. Hang in there.

LAURA HOUSE WAS TEACHING seventh grade in Austin, Texas, when she decided she'd rather be a comedian. She is now a regular performer/director at the Acme Comedy Theater in Hollywood and writes for TV shows like "George Lopez." You may have seen her on MTV's "Austin Stories" or playing a hillbilly slut opposite Natalie Portman in *Where the Heart Is.*

Rachel Resnick

Touch Me

IT'S BITINGLY COLD, YET here I am, naked under a nubby cotton sheet in Mexico about to get my first healing massage. A house call no less. I'm treating myself. Every year I make it through the holidays and past New Year's, a time dark with memories, it's cause for celebration. Joy, my host, said that BJ is rare, a natural born healer, that he comes and goes from San Miguel de Allende and does not live in one place. Grab the chance.

BJ is a big man with gorgeous Led Zeppelin hair and beautifully large hands. No wonder he's in demand. Dressed simply in baggy orange pants and a plain white T-shirt worn soft as if it's been washed a thousand times, he exudes a Buddha-like calm. This calmness is as big as his body. I'm about to shake his hand, but he fixes a steady gaze on me, and I forget what I was about to do.

Upstairs, in the guest bedroom where I'm staying, BJ moves around the portable massage table where I lie. The lights flick on, then off. The power's unpredictable here. So's the hot water. I've been chilled ever since I arrived in San Miguel a couple of weeks ago. My favorite thing to do on Christmas is to be in the air, losing the actual day in time zones and transit, so by the time I arrive at my destination, it's over. Then I'm in another country for New Year's, the most difficult time of all.

My breathing sounds unnaturally loud to me, and ragged. I must be anxious. I stare at a 3-D picture of the Virgin taped to the wall. This one's got dolorous brown eyes and a hot red mantilla. A few inches away, a bleached animal skull stares at me with empty eye sockets. Virgins and Death. So Mexico.

BJ rolls the sheet up and exposes my feet. Six p.m. Dusk. The hundred bells of San Miguel chime, peel, clang, ring, toll through the thin mountain air in mad randomness. When BJ touches me, my skin vibrates along with the crazy bells. What is it about a stranger's touch? The hourly cacophony sets off the birds with whom I share Joy's guest room. One cage holds two parakeets. The other cage holds three shy baby red-crowned Amazons. They chirrup and whistle and flap their tiny wings around the cages.

In between rescuing dogs and mentoring orphans, Joy bought and saved these birds from street sellers. Once they are grown, she will release them back into the wild. She is that kind of woman. I am not, though I'm not sure what kind of woman I am. Sometimes being motherless has that effect. You lack the blueprint. I think about the word *desmadres*, which literally means without mother, but also means mess.

BJ takes my feet in his hands. A vague panic stirs. "This is going to hurt," he says softly. "I want you to breathe through the pain." Even his voice radiates peace. Still, I feel my body stiffen. This doesn't feel like massage-as-pampering. Does he know the town's inquisitioner used to live four doors down? That a conquistador used to live here? Does he sense that this house, with its gracious twenty-foot ceilings and six-foot thick walls, is known to hold ghosts? A cold draft blows over me and I shiver.

Just as I'm about to talk, tell him about the former bullfighter-turned-love balladeer with the rainbow-painted motorcycle helmet I met in the square earlier, or ramble on about the ancient art of massage, or ask what it's like to be an ex-pat—my conversational gambits are as numerous as the town's bells—BJ wisely anticipates.

"It's best if you don't talk." This guy has my number.

He kneads my feet and it feels prayerful, even when he rocks his bony fists in the flat arches.

Then he moves his big hands onto my lower legs. And stays there. Goes deeper. Then deeper still. His hands now are shovels, picks, prying and parting dense muscle. Minutes later it feels like daggers spring from my shins, fire sprouts from my calves. Still he won't let up on my lower legs. I lose track of time. The pain flares, plunges. It's a matter of pride that I don't cry out. I couldn't talk if I wanted to. It's taking every ounce of concentration just to avoid saying, *"Stop. I can't stand it."*

Pain makes me hyper-aware. Every cell is at attention. The birds chirr, their tiny scaled feet scraping over birdseed and clanging quietly against cage wire. The rescue dogs bark. I hear meat bones flung on the cold tile floor down in the kitchen. The hollow thud, the scrabble of dog nails and even the slobber of their doggy mouths. But that's not possible. Is it? Unless the pain is sharpening my hearing. I can suck the cold in through my mouth, though my legs are aflame.

Under BJ's pressing, I feel my right thigh ripple under my kilt as I charge once again down the grass field in Cranford, New Jersey. I played center half, which meant I had license to chase you and smash your shins with my hockey stick to get the ball. I was living there because my mother lost custody. She couldn't take care of me anymore, so from age eleven I bounced from one home to another. I carried my aggression with me. In Alabama, where I moved with a foster family, I was captain of the school volleyball team, and a fearsome player on St. Andrew's Episcopal Church team, the Holy Terrors. Never mind I didn't then believe in God. I spiked the volleyball into people's faces until they cried for Jesus. No mercy. In college, I tackled a girl on the rugby field and sent her to the hospital with a split-open jaw. I can taste the old physical fury like a mouthful of *habanero.*

I'm not sure I can do this. How is this healing? I squeeze my eyes shut. BJ inexorably works his way up to my thighs, where the hurt intensifies. Pinwheels of pain spin out from thickly braided muscles. Spark and lift off. I white-knuckle the sides of the massage table. "Your right leg," BJ says, "is strong." He prods a thumb gently but determinedly into a bunched muscle. "Too much energy here. That can block flow. You need more *internal* strength."

Maybe. I've heard this before from yoga instructors. They, too, saw what I hid beneath my external strength; they saw my core was weak in comparison. More vulnerable. For years I built showy muscles, fed a violent drive.

"Let's turn you over," says BJ. I turn over. The sheet is wet with sweat. BJ drops a scratchy wool blanket on top, seeing my goosebumps. My legs are pulsing. Then it feels like BJ thrusts his hand directly into the center of my quad, hitting a hidden clump of electric tension. It's like he's unleashed grade VI whitewater rapids in there.

"Relax," BJ says. "Breathe." I do. My legs are churning, thrumming, stifling in their sheeted cocoon when all I want to do is run.

BJ plants his big hands on my back and instantly a new wave of pain begins. My proud back, with the ridge in the middle from years of crew and weightlifting. Knots of muscles lattice the ribs. Bowlines, monkey's fists, slipknots. I feel one of these knots unravel.

Joy has guilted me into joining her on the annual orphan girl outing to the Tuesday Mercado. At the end of the long day, I see myself kneeling in the chalky dust of the Mercado parking lot, tying one orphan girl's shoelaces on her beat-up boots. Earlier this orphan girl stuck her tongue out at me. She is stubborn, already hard-faced at eight years of age. The laces on her boots are dusty, cracked. The plastic tips are long gone, so it's hard to thread the ends; I find myself spitting into my hand to create a point for the bootlace. The boot is creased like a centurion's face. *My mother is on vacation*, the orphan girl says, clutching her plastic bags of cheap sweaters and sunglasses and *zapatos* to her side, looking directly at me with hooded eyes, like she's telling me a secret. *She's coming back.* And she grips her plastic bags tightly.

My brain shorts out as BJ presses on a knot. I am suddenly famished. Since arriving in Mexico, I have eaten green chorizo and gotten acute *turista*. I have eaten *nopales,* cactus. Picked up candy from a piñata busted at the stroke of midnight by a group of manic kids and eaten that, too. My hunger is inexhaustible. Now, as BJ digs into my shoulder blades, a sugary liqueur of sadness suffuses every vein, pumping sluggishly. That weight I bore on my shoulders, it falls, tumbles and bumps—rolls away into a corner like a sullen globe of the world.

I open my eyes for a moment. Pretty paper lanterns swing weirdly in the draft from an open window. Someone nearby puts on a record. Pedro Vargas. The sound is unbearably melancholic, warm and soulful. They say the bells of San Miguel were sweetened by gold, when the bell-maker melted down his dead lover's jewelry.

I am floating on the singer's notes. The almond-scented oil has simmered into my skin. I'm thinking we're done, I made it; I'm still a tough girl. Then BJ places his hands around my neck.

When I was in college, a woman with green tilted eyes and velveteen lashes gave me a gift certificate for a massage. This seemed an incredibly luxurious gift. How it happened, we were in her room smoking clove cigarettes, talking about Gertrude Stein, and then, on impulse, I told her about my mother. When she gathered me in her arms that night and held me on that narrow dorm bed and kissed my hair and neck, I fell in love. Love was more fluid then. Never mind we barely did anything. When she touched my thigh, I burned. I drove her to Cape Cod for a weekend to stay at Mrs. Fay's beachside guest cottage, thinking bravely, stupidly, this would be our time. Once during that weekend, when I was sitting on her lap and kissing her, she pushed me away. *What would Mrs. Fay say if she walked in now? Gee, er, Mrs. Fay, I really like my friend!* She was gay and did not want to be. I was not. I was just in love and free, then. I didn't care. You see, she reminded me of my mother. So when this woman picked up a coil of boat rope and wrapped it around her neck, and knotted it, and began tightening it, turning her neck red, saying, *I should just strangle myself*—her green eyes stubborn and glittering with what I realize in retrospect was intense homophobic panic—I freaked. I pleaded. Then I held her knees and laid my head by her feet for a very long time. Until she let the rope drop away.

After Cape Cod, this woman disappeared from my life. I never did use that gift certificate. I kept delaying, thinking: I'm not tired enough. I haven't worked hard enough. I haven't earned a massage yet. Maybe after finals. Maybe after crew season. Maybe in springtime. Until it expired.

I allow myself massages only when I'm traveling. In Shanghai, in a smoke-filled room lit only by an aquarium and the glow of cigarettes, I was massaged by a blind man with fingers like sea anemones; in Thailand, at the Temple of the Reclining Buddha, in a room decorated with gold, jam-packed with cots, a Thai man padded on my back, turning it into a bridge of flesh and conjuring ancient childhood trauma; in Tahiti, lush-hipped women rolled and stroked my skin with touches soft as the petals of a *tiare*.

I know that massage has the power to pull memory from muscle.

But even with my body a grid-work of pain, I was not prepared for what BJ did next in that freezing cold guest room in San Miguel.

⁂

BJ lightly touches my neck and for the first time that day I flinch. I wasn't expecting tenderness. I realize I've been braced for pain; that's easier. He pauses. I listen to him sigh softly. This is also the first time he's sighed. What is going on? My heart pounds. I feel his breath on my neck as he moves in closer. Then BJ digs his thumbs deep into my neck, and holds them there for a long time. Tears spring from the corners of my eyes, spill onto the cold tile floor. Slowly, he moves his fingers around and down, digging deep, circling the whole throat. Finally his fingers splay and grasp, cradle, and probe, all at once, as if tugging me by the very root of my skull, here into the fresh new world. Reborn. BJ says nothing, keeps working on my neck, though he sighs wearily. I don't know why, but this breaks my heart. Soon I am weeping. Gutbucket, racking sobs. In a way you never do in front of anyone. Let alone a stranger.

Or only a stranger. With anyone else, the stakes are too high. There is too much to lose with such exposure. Only a stranger. Or God.

For this is how my mother died: hanging herself by a rope tied around a beam in the attic of her parents' house in Dover, Massachusetts, on New Year's Eve, 1977. This year it will be 30 years since her death. Sometimes that feels like an eternity. Sometimes it feels like today.

❧ ❧ ❧

RACHEL RESNICK IS THE author of *Love Junkie: A Memoir* (Bloomsbury, 2008) and the *Los Angeles Times* bestseller, *Go West Young F*cked-Up Chick* (St. Martin's, 2000). She has published articles, essays, and celebrity-profile cover stories in the *Los Angeles Times*, *Women's Health*, and *BlackBook*, among others. She is a contributing editor at *Tin House* magazine. She is the founder and CEO of Writers on Fire, provider of luxury writing retreats both in the United States and abroad. Writers on Fire also offers private writing coaching and local (L.A.) workshops throughout the year. See *rachelresnick.com* and *writers.com* for more information.

Owen Egerton

Holiest of Times

THE HOURS ARE SLOW. My grandfather is not fully conscious, but we speak to him and read his favorite poems aloud. Occasionally he squeezes our hand or says a name. We, his family, are gathered in his small room in an assisted living home in west England.

It is a weird waiting, sitting by a deathbed. We fill the time by catching up on family gossip, watching cricket on television, passing my four-month-old baby back and forth and laughing at her babbling. In the early afternoon, we treat my grandmother to a pub lunch and a scenic drive. This is a routine we'll follow for the better part of a week.

Arden, our baby, is a star. We live in Texas so this is a first meeting for most of the family. In the evening after dinner, she shows off her newfound ability to put most of her foot into her mouth, rolling back and forth, gleefully sucking her toes as if they're sugarcoated. She giggles, she gurgles. She dozes, she whimpers. We sit around her in the same way we sit around my grandfather. Two nexuses of the family. One newly arrived. One preparing to leave. Both close to the edges of life. Both faces reflecting the pink-red glow of a low sun. One dawn and the other sunset. Both cry; both can only eat when fed; both call out in their sleep for their mothers.

My grandfather was born in Wales in 1913, before World Wars I and II, before the Holocaust, before television, international flights, computers. He didn't have electricity as a child. Arden was born in Austin, Texas, in 2005. Moments after breathing her first breath, photos of her were emailed via cell phone around the world. They are the oldest and the youngest, the chronological borders, of the family.

My grandfather had been at a hospital. I visited him there when we first arrived in England. It was a dim, clean room near a loud hallway. The nurses called him "Ivor," a name he hadn't answered to in decades. "He goes by Ken," I told them. They nodded and wrote nothing down. The doctors and nurses could not keep the tubes in Grandfather's arm. He pulled them out; he cried out through the night. They sent him back to his room at the assisted living home. Now there are no tubes, no doctors, and the attendants call him Ken. Except one, who insists on calling him "Poppet."

He does not need medication. He does not need doctors. He's not sick. He is dying.

Arden was born in a hospital. Florescent lights and the smell of disinfectant. Our doula, a birth guide, arrived shortly after we did. She lowered the lights and rubbed rich smelling oils on Jodi's legs. My wife, like my grandfather, frustrated the nurses and doctors by refusing their painkillers. Jodi was not sick. She was giving birth.

Our doula, Lanell, stayed with us throughout the birth, answering our questions with calm and encouraging words. The nurses and doctor checked in on us as labor progressed, but it was Lanell who remained close. As the contractions increased in strength, Jodi's eyes opened wide. Her expression seemed to be asking, "Is my body doing this right? Should I be afraid?" Lanell took her hand. "You're doing great," she said and smiled. "Your body is doing just what it should be doing." Jodi nodded and took some deep breaths.

My mother acts as doula for her father, guiding him through an experience easily as strange and intense as birth. She often leans close to him and reminds him we are here. She gives him sips of water and tells him he is doing fine. She is not telling him that he is making a recovery. That would be a lie. Instead she assures him, with spoken and unspoken gestures, that it's all right to let go.

Only once during the days around my grandfather's bed does he open his eyes, although he is urged often. I believe he opens his eyes not for his sake but for ours. We believe we are there for him. And I imagine he is grateful enough, but the truth is we are there for our own reasons. He is working on deeper things. He is speaking to friends and relatives long since dead, mumbling their names from a dry mouth. He is visiting places he hasn't seen since he was a child. For him the lines are thin: between what is and what was, between the living and the dead. Who are we to interrupt such journeys so he can acknowledge our presence?

Perhaps it is not as spiritual as I would describe. Perhaps it's a brain melting away, confused and full of dementia. Or maybe it is both. A note from a guitar is a floating moment of music and also simply a vibrating string. I'm told my baby's first smile was just a rumble in her belly. But it pierced my heart nonetheless.

My parents, both doctors, can see my grandfather's death approaching stage by stage. They estimate the days and later hours, monitoring his progression in the same way that, months before, they had felt Jodi's belly and described the baby's development. There are no real surprises as my grandfather lies in his bed. He is traveling a well-worn path. New for him, but as old as life. He does hold on a day or two longer than my parents had suspected. "He's always been stubborn," my mother says. Her brothers smile. My grandfather has crept up to the edge of death, and like a prolonged labor, he holds strong and moves not an inch forward. We wait, taking turns holding his hand, taking turns walking with the baby in the garden.

Then, on the day before my family is scheduled to fly home, a change in breath and skintone tell my parents that his passing will be in the next ten minutes or so. The family quickly gathers around his bed; my mother takes her father's hand and speaks gentle words as if she is calming a child to sleep. My grandmother kisses his lips and speaks his name. We watch those stuttered last breaths. Then he stops breathing all together. He is dead. And the strange thing is, it's a surprise. Has this just happened? But it most certainly has. There's a change in the room as clear as the first winds of a storm front.

The moment of Arden's birth was preempted by hours of labor, the drama of pushing, the excitement of seeing the crown of her head. But here, too, the moment of birth was a surprise. There's a photo of Jodi and me first seeing the baby. Our faces are bright with shocked amazement, as if a baby was the last thing we expected to see.

When my grandfather, Poppa is what we call him, when Poppa dies, the staff of the home lets us sit with him. Touch him. My grandmother kisses his cheek one last time. They leave us for as long as we need. It is holy and odd. I'm reminded of our first hours with Arden, refusing the nurse's offer to take her to the nursery. We held her: a small, warm creature with the smell of birth still on her new skin. Later Jodi would comment on how amazing it is that people were working, shopping, or just hanging out while something as extreme as birth was happening.

And didn't we feel that leaving my grandfather's room? How dare there be a sitcom playing on television. How dare two men argue outside the window or a dog bark at birds in the yard. Quiet. My grandfather died today.

All this holiness hiding in a corner of the world, in a corner of the day. I find myself afraid of the holy. The same fear that fills my belly when I look out over a canyon or stand alone in the dark. It takes a certain effort to sit still. There's a desire to let the attendants push us out of my grandfather's room, let the nurses take the baby, let some official, authoritative hand fill the moment with the "necessary." The moments—quiet with a new life, quiet with a passed life—whisper too loudly. The gain, the loss, the change. The moments remind us of our own condition, and we fear that if we listen too closely the horrible awe of it all will break us.

In spite of our fear, we do listen to what the holy is whispering. We sat with the baby. We sit with the body. It doesn't break us, but it changes us.

When my wife and I return from England both of us follow the lessons in different directions. Jodi begins volunteering at a local hospital visiting new mothers and speaking with them about breast-feeding, basic baby health and ways to connect with other mothers. She especially enjoys helping the younger mothers, teenage girls with frightened eyes and homework due. Jodi also begins her training to be a doula herself. I'm drawn to the other end of the journey and start volunteering with a local hospice group. I sit with the dying, usually in their homes. Sometimes we talk about life and spirit. Sometimes baseball and the best way to make a milkshake. Often there's no talk at all. At night Jodi and I compare notes and are continually intrigued by the parallels of blessings and pains experienced by families losing a loved one or birthing a child. These two moments—life beginning and life ending—offer brief, often startling, glimpses into the nature of what it means to be human.

Arden is in the room when her great-grandfather dies. She quietly nurses in her mother's arms. Her eyes are closed and there is a question in her tiny brow. When my grandmother cries, she stops nursing and cries as well.

Later that night, after many tears, I place Arden in my grandmother's lap. My grandmother's gaze, which had been glazed and distant, focuses on the baby. She cradles her in her thin hands and leans close. She wipes her own eyes and smiles. Arden smiles back and laughs a little. My grandmother also laughs. Arden reaches out and touches my grandmother's face as the family sits still, holding the moment and feeling the holy.

❧ ❧ ❧

OWEN EGERTON IS THE author of the novel *Marshall Hollenzer is Driving* and the short story collection *How Best to Avoid Dying*. He is also an accomplished screenplay writer and commentator for NPR affiliated stations. He is the co-creator of the award-winning comedy hit "The Sinus Show," and for several years he was the artistic director of Austin's National Comedy Theatre. Egerton earned his MFA in Creative Writing from Texas State University in 2005. He currently lives in Austin, Texas, with his wife and two children.

David Zuniga

The Truth Remains

The master asked his students,
"What happens to a Buddha when he dies?"
The elder student answered,
"Nothing. When a Buddha dies nothing remains."
The master smiled and replied, "No, the truth remains."

I HAVE BEEN IN end-of-life healthcare for almost ten years, and as an interfaith chaplain I have talked with literally thousands of terminally ill patients and grieving family members after a loved one has died. I have worked with both children and adults, in medical settings ranging from chaotic emergency rooms to serene hospices. But one of the saddest encounters I have had involved a woman whose cancer was actually cured.

The patient and her husband were in their mid-fifties, and she had dutifully come to all her surgery, chemotherapy, and radiation treatments. She had completed her treatment and was there for a follow-up appointment when I walked into her room at the clinic and found her alone, crying inconsolably. She was always very strong and since the doctor had just told her the news that all cancer patients long to hear—that her cancer had not come back—I assumed she would be elated.

I sat down next to her and gently asked her what was wrong. "My husband has never been there for me. All these long years he could never just sit with me; he could never listen to me, to my feelings, as I was going through this," she cried.

I was shocked. Her husband had always seemed jovial and friendly, and yet, as is so often the case in human relations, there is always something deeper. When I asked why her husband had been unsupportive she told me that several years ago their teenage son had been killed by a drunk driver. "My husband would never grieve. He would never share his feelings with anyone. He just shut down. I miss our son, too. But you can't give up; you have to face the situation directly and you have to go on."

We talked for a long time that afternoon. Mostly I tried to provide a supportive and compassionate listening presence. I knew I could not take away all of her suffering. Instead, I walked with her as far and as fully as I could.

Tragically, her husband was caught in a deep state of *samsara*. Most religions define suffering as a form of sin, as being separated from God. In Buddhism we refer to suffering as *samsara*, which translated from Sanskrit literally means journeying. *Samsara*, suffering, is a cyclical state of existence whereby one clings to destructive practices and attitudes, often making the situation even worse than it has to be. To liberate one's self and others from suffering is one of the main points of Buddhist practice.

Losing a child is unimaginably difficult and I have nothing but compassion for this grieving father. But his wife was right; her husband had never faced the truth of their son's death and consequently he was caught in a deep state of *samsara*. He had not learned to deal with death, so it haunted him, causing him to sink into deeper and deeper states of suffering. Suffering can tear our hearts open and in the process make us more compassionate and wise and thereby help us to transform the suffering in our own lives and the lives of others. Or suffering can tear us apart, making us apathetic, fearful, and angry. This man's son had died and many years later he could not be there for his wife when she needed him the most. As his wife observed, "That night it wasn't just our son who died. My husband died, too, and I feel like I am all alone."

Another key principal in Buddhist philosophy in relation to suffering is the law of *karma*. In the west, *karma* is often presented as a nebulous and esoteric force of spiritual justice. Translated from Sanskrit, *karma* literally means deed or action. Contrary to the way it is often depicted, *karma* is actually a very humanistic, rational principal. To analyze someone's *karma* is to look deeply into the causes and conditions of their life, what makes them who they are, what events shaped them into the current moment of their existence, much as a psychologist or psychiatrist might analyze someone's life to help them discern causal patterns and liberate them from destructive cycles. This grieving father and husband surely had some profound *karmic* losses, some tragic events in his life, which led him to a place where he could not deal with either the loss of his son or his wife's illness.

Guilt has no place here, as indeed guilt has no place anywhere on the true religious path. The only skillful response for this man is compassion—compassion because both he and his wife are suffering. Certainly he was not behaving kindly towards his wife. Sadly, chronic illnesses and death often bring out the very worst in people. But it is important to remember that when people inflict great suffering on others, they, too, are suffering in some profound way, trapped by deep delusion. There are causes and conditions for all things; this is the law of *karma*. The skillful step is not to sit in judgment, but rather to look deeply into the patterns and events that led up to the current situation. In this way, one can act skillfully to ease the pain of all who are suffering.

It is easy to have compassion for this man because we all labor under what is perhaps the greatest cultural delusion of all: We deny death. Our society is a death-denying society. Death is one of the last taboo topics. It is the one universal constant that cuts across all racial, cultural, and religious divides and it is also the least acknowledged phenomenon of human existence. So it is easy to see why people react with denial and other unskillful coping mechanisms when faced with the great matter of our inevitable death. This is a tragedy because the only way to overcome suffering is to face it directly. Many are taught that if they just pray hard enough, if they just have enough religious faith, they can overcome anything. But if we view death as something to be conquered then we are ultimately doomed to lose.

A key facet of Zen practice is non-discriminating consciousness: Everything comes from the mind. In the West, we tend to think happiness and suffering are contingent on external circumstances. But happiness and suffering are never solely in the event itself, rather, they are cultivated by our consciousness. When confronted with great suffering, our tendency is to plead and bargain. We fruitlessly live in a state of denial, thinking someone or something else can save us. This is why Siddhartha Gautama, the historical Buddha, declared, "Make an island of yourself, make yourself your refuge; there is no other refuge" (*Digha Nikaya* 16). Through Zen practice we see and experience directly that the key to liberation from suffering lies within.

Most of the time our mind is like a monkey frantically leaping from tree to tree, never able to stop and rest. We cling to things we deem as good although they will inevitably change; we fiercely resist things we deem as bad although we often have much less control than we think; and we tend to tune out most of the rest of our existence. With this non-stop monkey mind it is easy to see why people are so distracted and fail to recognize the beauty that is all around them. The great tragedy is not that we die but that we never fully live. In my end-of-life work I have seen little children, seemingly cheated of life, die with joyfulness and equanimity, and I have seen adults in their eighties die with anger, fear, and regret. As the historical Buddha observed, "Better it is to live one day virtuous and meditative than to live a hundred years immoral and uncontrolled" (*Dhammapada* 110). Therefore the key is not how long we live, but rather how mindfully we live.

Our materialistic consumer society does not lend itself to mindful living, yet living mindfully is our only salvation. Mindfulness is a term that is employed in a wide array of ways in pop culture—most of them off the mark. The Pali word *sati* is translated into English as mindfulness, and *sati* style meditation was a hallmark of ancient Buddhism twenty-five hundred years ago, and it is practiced in the same way to this day. The mindfulness method of meditation is generally practiced through focusing on one of four objects: the body, feelings, mind, and the objects of mind. In the process, our whole orientation to ourselves, others, and even death itself is radically transformed. For example, we are conditioned to believe that our mind, the seat of our consciousness, makes us a fixed, autonomous, distinct, discreet, individual "self." But when we focus on our mind through *sati*, through mindfulness meditation, we experience directly how our minds are not fixed, individual "selves" but rather ever changing processes and continuums of experience. Like clouds drifting across the sky we learn to observe with equanimity and delight, yet not cling to, all the slings and arrows that tend to besiege human existence.

Just as meditation liberates us from our attachments, it frees us from our constricting and limiting sense of selfhood. Our minds, our bodies, and indeed everything in the universe exists in this eternal ebb and flow of change. We are all interconnected, hence the common meditation mantra: "No birth, no death." As Albert Einstein declared, "I feel myself so much a part of everything living that I am not the least concerned with the beginning or ending of the concrete existence of any one person in this eternal flow."

While it is certainly important to have a steady meditation practice, all things in life can be meditation and hence ripe opportunities for transformation. This is why we say Zen is chopping wood and carrying water. Our very life is our religious practice. Whether you are changing the diaper of your baby or working in the garden, whether you are seasoning vegetables in your kitchen or taking your last breaths before going into surgery, every moment of your life should be approached mindfully. In meditation we hone our mind into pure, direct awareness. All physical and mental events become revealed as interconnected parts of an eternally changing continuum. When we die to our small sense of self, the narrow and confining "I", then the infinite and unified "We" of the universe is revealed and we are liberated from our fear of death.

"Zen" is derived from the Sanskrit work *dhyana* which literally means absorption. This *dhyana* style of meditation spread to China and was called *Ch'an-na* or *Ch'an*. As it moved down the Korean peninsula it was called *Son-na* or *Son*, and when it eventually came to Japan from Korea, it was pronounced *Zen-na* or Zen, which is the most commonly used term in the West for this meditation style.

This *dhyana* or Zen meditative state yields profound and abiding states of quiescence and stillness whereby the practitioner can sit untroubled and undisturbed by situations which would shatter most people. This serenity amidst distress is exemplified by Kwaisen, the abbot of Yerin-ji in 1582. When Kwaisen refused to turn over soldiers he was protecting, his temple was set on fire. Facing imminent death he asked each of his students how they should live out the last fleeting moments of their lives. Each of them responded in their own way and then he declared, "For peaceful meditation, we need not go to the mountains and streams. When thoughts are quiet, fire itself is cool and refreshing." And thus in their moment of death they were liberated from all anger and fear.

The story of Kwaisen reveals a profound truth about the great matter of death. Zen philosophy is deep and lovely, but the marrow of Zen is realized through meditation. There is no substitute; practice is always of supreme importance. And meditation is not limited to when we sit on a cushion in a zendo. Everything we do should be meditation. And in this way we welcome even our difficulties because they are our great teachers.

Zen is frequently depicted as a spiritual path of being solely in the present moment. But the wisdom of Zen transcends mere distinctions of the past, present, and future. Thus Siddhartha Gautama taught, "Let go of the past, let go of the future, let go of the present, and cross over to the farther shore of existence. With mind wholly liberated, you shall come no more to birth and death" (*Dhammapada* 348). As Zen practitioners we don't just let go of the past and future, we let go of even the present moment. To let go of the present moment is to transcend our attachment to even ourselves, to life itself. Everything is constantly changing. Nothing exists in a fixed, eternal state. When we cling to things we inevitably suffer because nothing remains unchanged.

This acknowledgement of change does not mean we become apathetic or disinterested in life. The Zen path is an immersion in both the joys and sorrows of existence. When we are healthy we appreciate our health, when we are sick we are transformed by our illness. And either way we are mindful that everything is constantly changing. Liberated from attachments we are able to sit fully with the entire range of human existence.

A legendary monk named Bodhidharma who is said to have brought the *dharma*, the teachings of Buddhism, from India to China is said to have offered a four part definition of Zen as: 1. A special transmission outside the orthodox teaching, 2. Nondependence on sacred writings, 3. Direct pointing to the human heart, 4. Realization of one's own nature and becoming a Buddha. There is much wisdom in this explication of Zen. One of the key concepts in Bodhidharma's transmission of Zen is that Zen is a truth that lies beyond words, symbols, and language. Words are never the thing in and of themselves. At best they are but poor players, fingers pointing at the moon, but they are never the moon itself.

Three months ago (as of this writing) my daughter was born. Before that, the last baby I had held was as a chaplain in a morgue. I washed and prepared the tiny body for it to be seen one last time by the devastated parents. These two events may seem far removed from one another, yet birth and death occur everyday. And even the greatest poets, philosophers, writers, and thinkers can never fully convey the raw emotions of the birth of a baby or the death of someone we love. If language is not even able to fully capture events which happen every day, it certainly cannot encapsulate the highest realizations of the religious path.

The problem with most religious beliefs is that they are rooted in language and concepts, yet language and concepts can never fully express the deepest spiritual truths. In Zen, we take the opposite approach; instead of cultivating belief we actively cultivate great doubt. This approach was illustrated by one of my brother priests a few years ago. As my friend Ilmee Sunim was traveling through India he came upon a funeral service on the Ganges river. As he sat in meditation watching the body be cremated on the funeral pyre the great question occurred to him: "What happens to us when we die?" As he shared this story with me a beautiful smile conveyed his spiritual realization, "I realized that I have no idea what happens to us when we die!" The truth is no one knows what will happen to us when we die. We do not even know what will happen to us tomorrow when we get out of bed, much less what happens when our physical life ends. Embracing the not-knowingness of life is where real religious wisdom lies.

This is why in Zen we say great doubt equals great enlightenment. There is so much in life that we do not know. Instead of clinging to words and concepts, can we honestly face the fact that we do not know the answer to so many great questions? Can we radically embrace things precisely the way they are; can we face reality unclouded by fear, attachment, and delusion?

Death is the ultimate teacher. It teaches us gratitude and illuminates our interconnection with all sentient beings. When we deny our mortality we are truly dead. When we face our death directly, we learn to live fully in every moment of our precious existence. This is why, in the *Mahaparinirvana Sutra*, the Buddha referred to facing death as the supreme form of meditation.

Most people die as they live. If we face life unafraid, openly and honestly, we will be empowered to die in the same way and our death will be transformative. But if we live life clouded by mental poisons such as anger and fear, we will die the same way, bitter and defeated.

In our society we spend so much time clinging and grasping, trying to accumulate things which will inevitably change. All the while we ignore our mortality, the supreme truth of our existence. This is why Dogen Zenji proclaimed, "Great is the matter of birth and death. All is impermanent, quickly passing. Awake! Awake each one. Don't waste this life."

DAVID ZUNIGA IS THE first westerner to be ordained as a priest in the Taego Order, the largest lineage of Korean Zen, and is the third Buddhist to be licensed as a professional chaplain. David has worked in pediatric and adult end-of-life healthcare for several years. He earned a Master of Divinity from Harvard, holds an MA in English literature, and is currently pursuing a Ph.D. in clinical psychology at the Fielding Institute. He is the former co-director of the Harvard Buddhist Community and has published several articles on religion in both the United States and Asia. He is the founder of the Metta Zen Center. David is married and has a young daughter. He enjoys the martial arts and ultra-running.

Jim Krusoe

Memorial—for L.H.

ONCE UPON A TIME I bought a pup, and because he liked to run, I got in the habit of driving up into the mountains every morning to let him race around for an hour or so while I walked after him. It was a crazy habit, what with the drive taking at least thirty minutes there and another thirty back, sometimes longer than the walk itself, and when I think about it now, I realize I was probably having some sort of low-grade nervous breakdown. Then, there was the waste of gas, the pollution I was creating, the miles put on my van, and even the fact that once, returning from one of those trips in the pouring rain, my van slid into a brand new BMW, which cost something, too. But I don't think I ever missed a day, and maybe it was cheaper than therapy.

It was on one of those mornings that I noticed a small bamboo cross, about four feet tall and two feet wide, that had been stuck into a pile of stony debris at the foot of a cliff, and my first thought was that children had been playing there. A couple of days later when I returned, the cross was spray-painted black, and someone had left a few dried flowers at its base. It was for a pet—a cat, I guessed—though I couldn't figure out why anyone would have gone all that distance just to bury a cat, and certainly the spot, a mass of rocks and pebbles, wasn't the easiest place to dig a hole. Time passed—a week, maybe two. I got a speeding ticket, adding eighty-five dollars to the cost of the walks, and when I finally returned to the spot, to my surprise there was a heavy six-foot wooden cross, freshly sawed and bolted together, stuck like a stake into the ground. I revised my theory. It couldn't have been for a cat. Instead I figured this was the meeting place of some renegade Christian sect. Still, I couldn't think of any reason why they would have to gather in such a difficult place to get to.

Weeks passed. I think the Christmas holidays went by, and I had extra time in the mornings to drive even farther away for our walks, so it wasn't until mid-January that I returned to the site to find the cross still there, set by then in a base of poured concrete, the flowers put in pots. At the foot of the cross was a plaque that read, "At this site Javier Hernandez fell to his death," followed by the dates of his birth and his fall. He had been fourteen, and all around the cross were careful notes on lined school paper from his friends describing their holidays, the parties they'd gone to, the presents they'd gotten, and telling how much they missed him. The one I remember most, as if the boy's death had rendered him suddenly all-knowing and impossibly finicky, ended: "I'm sorry for my bad spelling. Your friend, Jose."

What kept me thinking about it though—or at least what I think keeps me thinking about it—is the question of where we go to mourn the ones we loved. Why, for example, had Javier's friends and family picked the place where he died rather than visit the cemetery to leave their stream of messages? Did they imagine that all alone in that ancient land of dark and wandering souls, perhaps out of some sense of familiarity, Javier had chosen to hang around the spot where he had entered? Did his family leave notes at the cemetery as well, just to be on the safe side?

❧ ❧ ❧

About thirty years ago I visited a house on a dusty street in a small village in Mexico where a poet, Lopez Velarde, lived and died. The place was exactly as if he still lived there, with only the addition of a guest book and an old lady to watch it and a few commemorative paintings. My favorite was one of the poet as a somber, middle-aged man. In it, his back was turned to a set of French doors and a wide green lawn, maybe symbolizing eternity, and next to him was a heaping plate of half-eaten, brightly colored Mexican pastries.

I had come to Mexico to stay with a friend, Jean-Phillip Carson, whose house was on that same street. He sold his home in Los Angeles about the time Nixon bombed Cambodia, saying he couldn't stand sending his taxes to such a government. J-P had owned a big, beautiful dog, an Akita, and the man and the dog formed one of those couples that famously resembled each other. Both were sleek, had tiny, even rows of teeth, and mutton chop whiskers. Though the dog had been hit by a truck a couple months earlier, in a freak accident in a town about fifty miles to the north, whenever the two of us passed a certain part of the street where another dog used to bark at his, J-P and I would cross over, as if his dog were still alive. It was J-P's habit to lie flat out on the living room rug each afternoon, and he said that when the dog was alive the dog would join him. Then, the afternoon of the day before I was to leave, J-P took his nap as usual, but when he came out from the room his face was wet. He said he had a dream in which his dog came to him, this dog he had loved so much, but when he reached out to touch him, the dog's eyes had changed into the eyes of a wolf. "Why would that make me cry?" he asked me, his face still gleaming. "That's the strangest part of it," he said. "Stranger by far than the dream."

I left him and took the long and scenic route back to Los Angeles. J-P was supposed to leave about ten days later, drive up quickly, and meet me to resume a discussion we had begun in Mexico about his founding a magazine devoted to images on film—something I was completely unqualified for, but which I fantasized would change my life. I dawdled along the coast, spent some extra time in San Diego, and when I arrived in Los Angeles, there was an airmail letter waiting for me. It said that in order not to pass through the town where his dog had been killed, J-P had taken another route, one on which a cattle truck had been forced to brake suddenly, flipping over onto his small car. He had died instantly on the road between Mazatlan and Culican, near one of those spots along the highway I used to see covered by clusters of small crosses indicating accidents and put there in memory of others who had died.

❧ ❧ ❧

And all of this came back to me the other night when I dreamed of a man who died a while ago—a writer, an editor, and an uneasy friend by the name of Lee Hickman. In my dream, Lee started out as the Lee I knew: brilliant, painfully self-conscious, looking as always like a boy whose mother dressed him, a character out of one of those fifties comedies, a Junior or Ricky or a Bud, now grown-up and gotten terribly off-track, too wise and cynical and sad and needy ever to coax laughs out of a live studio audience. Then Lee began to change his shape, going from old to young, from one person to another (although I always knew it was Lee) and finished up as Michel Foucault.

This wasn't quite as odd as it might sound, because throughout his life Lee had always wanted to be my teacher, and though I certainly needed one, for various not-very-good reasons, I resisted. In almost any group of writers we would find ourselves sitting on opposite sides of the room, as far apart as possible, yet of course, staring at each other. Now after his death I found myself in my dream needing to ask his opinion. "Lee," I said, "I've been writing these essays and I don't think they're the least smart in a way that you'd like them." (Lee's magazine had prided itself on its post-modernly distance and poetry.) "But to tell the truth, they seem to be the best that I can manage."

I waited for the Lee in my dream to answer while he took his time changing back from Foucault to himself. "Well . . ." he shrugged, and then gave a sort of tired wave as if he'd either given up or just didn't care. Meanwhile, I watched as he began to fade, like a released fish traveling deeper and deeper beneath the surface, back to join the other dead, where he still lives, not unclearly as in life—that drawer full of snapshots constantly being shuffled—but inside my mind, becoming simpler with each passing day: a phrase, a word, a syllable, and finally just a sound—a howl for all those ever lost and for all those soon to be.

❧ ❧ ❧

JIM KRUSOE HAS PUBLISHED two books of short stories, five books of poetry, and two novels, *Iceland* (Dalkey Archive) and *Girl Factory* (Tin House Books). His next novel, *Erased,* is scheduled for publication by Tin House in 2009.

Marie Wilson

The Three-Legged Dog

AT 4:54 A.M. ON April 4, 1984, Clifford Wallace Wilson, our "baby bear," announced his presence to the world. As I looked at my precious son, the clarity of becoming a mother overwhelmed me and, at the same time, filled my heart with joy. So began the glorious journey of mother and child—the miracle of discovery, the joy of hearing "mommy" for the first time, seeing him take his first steps, and so many other wonderful "firsts." I was in love with my son; he was the light of my life.

Days slipped into months and months into years. Before I knew it, Cliff had grown into a young man. It was May 2002 and I could hardly believe it was time for him to graduate and head off to college. We were very proud of him. He was excited to start his new life. I, already wistful at his pending departure, felt anxious. On his graduation day I handed him this poem:

It Seems Like Yesterday
A Graduation Poem for My Dear Son

It seems like yesterday that you were sleeping in my arms,
An angel's face with a baby's charm.

It seems like yesterday you took your first steps, first rode a bike,
Played t-ball and soccer and flew your first kite.

Was it that long ago when I bandaged your knee from a fall?
I remember when you could barely crawl!

It seems like yesterday when we took our cabin trips,
When we rode the Rio Frio in a blow-up boat,
Paddling with nary a care.
It seems like yesterday that we were there.

Enchanted Rock, pumpkin carving, egg dyeing, Disney World,
Trips to grandma and grandpa's, bedtime stories of Mr. Bibilibob.
It seems like yesterday but now you are grown,
My fine, handsome young son,
I am so proud to call you my own.

Those cherished memories flash before me like a picture show and,
Today I want you to know I cherish those memories made,
Your lessons learned and honors earned.

Today I want you to know that I wish you bright new dreams,
And beautiful sights you have yet to see.

Today I want you to know that I wish you joy and happiness
In all that you are yet to be!

It seems like yesterday…a blink of an eye,
But eighteen years have gone by and with bittersweet tears,
Today I wish you only the best Tomorrows!

I love you dearly, Mom

As a graduation present, I planned a trip to Canada. Cliff and I toured New Brunswick and Prince Edward Island together. We made some fabulous memories—kayaking, hiking, horseback riding, and whale watching. We did it all, including riding our bikes through a downpour. The day of the rainstorm we rode back to our B&B soaking wet, and Cliff said undeterred, "This was the best day ever, Mom."

In December 2002, Cliff finished his first semester at college and was home for the holidays. It was wonderful to see him and before I knew it he was back on the road to start his second semester. And I, too, was off to spend a long vacation with family in Florida.

I was still there on February 2, 2003, when the phone rang at 11:30 p.m. Larry, my boyfriend calling from Texas, haltingly informed me that, "There was a tragic car accident. Cliff didn't make it."

Clifford Wallace Wilson arrived in heaven two months shy of his nineteenth birthday and all that I had envisioned for my precious son was stripped away in an instant.

My two sisters accompanied me home. And so it began—we relived that moment over and over with family and friends who gathered to rally around. And as we painfully made the funeral arrangements, chose the flowers, and selected music, it all seemed surreal. All thc while, praying to God to please send my boy home...please, just come home!

His body returned to us. My son was in a coffin! This was the least real of all...*not him!* This was not Cliff! The overwhelming sadness and tears never seemed to end. This was a moment I wanted to rewind...fix...start over...change the outcome of, but I was totally out of control. I continuously recalled the evening of the dreaded news when I lay in bed, clutching my son's picture to my heart. My light was gone; my heart was broken.

As it was in the early years, now, in his passing, a series of "firsts" began. First birthday without him, first Mother's Day... every holiday was filled with pain.

One morning, in the depths of despair, I suddenly envisioned a picture of a three-legged dog. In fact I was very much like this dog: out of balance, missing an integral part, unable to move forward.

Another anniversary approached, this time an annual 5K race Cliff had run in for several years. Cliff enjoyed participating in various 5Ks with his family. He had left me in the dust many times. In fact, I had not done the race for a few years because of a bothersome knee. This year I could not let this race pass without entering.

Larry and I began at the starting line, hand in hand, with pictures of Cliff pinned on our backs. As I looked to my left, there, just beside me, was a three-legged dog eager to run despite his loss. I heard Cliff's voice then—I don't mean I imagined it; I mean I heard it: *You can do it, Mom! I know you can carry on just like the three-legged dog; you have work to do.*

We finished the race in Cliff's honor. As we drove home, I continued to think of the three-legged dog. I knew that I needed to continue my life's race, proudly and joyfully, in memory of my son and for my son. I did not magically set my grief down in that moment, but I turned a corner, something shifted, and I knew I had to start moving forward.

That Christmas I sent candles to family members and wrote:

Forever Bright
In Memory of our Beloved Cliff
December 2003
Although we can't hold you near,
We forever carry you in our hearts so dear.
Our love for you is a common bond,
As we remember your beautiful smile,
You will always live on.
You have touched so many lives; this is clear.
The loss of your goodness, your wit, your charm,
We miss you my son and wish you were here.
But, for now, we shall gather your memories around the light,
Like the love in our hearts forever bright.
Your spirit surrounds us in this place,
Till the day we all join hands and see your beautiful face.

In September 2004, I was packing to return home from a trip to Wyoming visiting a friend who had also lost a child. That whole day I was feeling melancholy. Going home was a reminder that I had to face the fact that Cliff would not be there; I could not share my trip experiences with him. I would not see his smiling face and experience his energy and excitement about my trip. As we headed out to the airport, a three-legged dog came running out of a neighbor's house towards the car and I was reminded of Cliff's voice that day of the race: *You can do this, Mom!*

In October 2006, more than three years after losing Cliff, I decided I needed to step out of my comfort zone and go on a trip with some women from a local women's group, none of whom I knew. In the past this was not a problem, but it had become one. After the loss of my son I had become more withdrawn.

Heading to the first planning meeting I grew anxious and began a list of reasons to back out of the trip. I approached the meeting place unsure of myself. As I entered the room, a three-legged dog greeted me. His name was Chance.

❧ ❧ ❧

In the five years since Cliff's death, I have continued to move forward, not always with ease, but always one foot at a time. Along the way, I have come to know my grief very well, and this has become my truth:

- I will have good days and I will have days when grief will overwhelm me.
- I need to continue to memorialize my son in the form of helping others in his name.
- I know that I need to continue to talk about Cliff.
- I know that I need to take care of myself.
- I know that at times I must tell others what I need.
- I know that without faith, family, and friends I could not make it.
- I also know that sometimes I just need some space and time.
- I have committed to live life for the both of us; I guess I have a lot of work to do!

I know that this empty space in my heart will always be here. It is by no means easy, but I also know that what I choose to do about it is what matters. Like the three-legged dog, I will carry on.

My prayer for myself and for those who have lost a dear one is to recognize what their next step is and to pay attention with all of their heart to the messages that come their way, because there will be signs that are not just coincidences...perhaps even your own three-legged dog!

MARIE WILSON, BORN IN Brooklyn, New York, has resided in Austin, Texas, since June of 1984. Marie is a published writer and owner of Method to Your Madness, a firm specializing in professional organizing and administrative support since 1997. She has recently received her real estate license, and she is a CASA volunteer and a choir member at Riverbend Church. Health and fitness is key, so Marie enjoys routine exercise, gardening, and kayaking; she is a member of the Texas Outdoors Woman Network. Marie loves to read, travel, and spend time with her family in Florida and New Jersey.

Donnalyn Watt

I Cannot Think What To Do

THERE ARE NO MORE paper bags under the kitchen sink, no more removable stereo speaker facades, no more VHS tapes in the top of the closet behind the winter sweaters. All of my husbands have been stashers of containers, pot, or porn. They are all gone. There are also no more late nights listening for her curfew, sewing sequins on dance costumes, or hours of conversation. My daughter is off to college. My son has been gone for years. Out in the world finding their way with little need of my presence, my children seem like shadows in my heart. My husbands, in comparison, have hardly left an impression. My daughter has better manners than my son but our relationship is no deeper, perhaps a bit kinder, so I see her often for a quick meal or some shopping. I am oddly attentive to her every facial expression, trying to make a minute of our time together last longer than sixty seconds. In these same moments she seems so casual, as if she is just passing through.

My house feels oddly large and missing its owner. You'd think that I would have adjusted by now. I haven't been married in over a decade and my daughter is starting her sophomore year. In this last year, I realize that there is another mistake to add to the very long list of my lifetime of mistakes. I have miscalculated again. I finished graduate school in my daughter's senior year of high school. Empty nesters generally explore new learning, or travel, or volunteer, or pickup an old interest so that this transition from a family to a single person might be more palatable. And they use these coping tools after the last child has left, not while the child is still in the home as I did. That year, my master's degree finished, my therapist said that I was a little ahead of schedule and I misinterpreted this, thinking being ahead, as a positive position. At that time, I think, I have escaped and since I was not in overt pain, I believed that I processed this transition with the wisdom of foresight. After all, I am where I have always wanted to be.

During the week I leave my house extra early and come home extra late to beat the traffic into town and miss it on the way out of town, but really to limit my time at home. On the weekends I tell myself I am going to get coffee and then return home directly to clean or finish projects but instead I drive around the Hill Country for most of the day making up lives that I might want based on fence lines and commercial opportunities of the small store fronts. I try to think of things that I could make that someone would want to buy. I leave my house with papers and books piled high. Clothing lies where it was hastily dropped on my way to sleep or bathe. I yearn to move my body and my mind to a place of passionate intention, like the focus of parenting or completing college or learning a new partner. I cannot think what to do. And then I begin to feel the heartache.

I have gained thirty pounds in the year since my last family members' exit into the greater world. Milkshakes, queso, chocolate frosting: any foods that are thick with fat and sugars and ooze down my throat filling me with the warm full numbness of sedation. This new body is uncomfortable, undressable, and in my mind unlovable. It is also exhausted. I feel torn between physical impulses to run while simultaneously I fight an urge to lie down. This constant physical conflict is disorienting, matching the geography or lack of geography of the days that I agree to enter into each morning. This agreement is always tentative and quite last minute. I sit at the highway intersection that leaves my small town towards my city job. One left turn and I am on my way to work. A right turn and I am on open highway traveling towards what has reluctantly become the familiarity of the unknown.

I am not overtly distressed but I am disoriented. At night I stand in my backyard, mosquitoes biting my ankles, looking at the stars surprised that I don't fall into space. I am also dismayed by the recollection of times when I wished for a quiet single existence. No one ever said congratulations on your pregnancy and the decision to forfeit your life. I didn't realize that after thirty years of parenting that I would end up at the edge of a wide-open space, angry, not knowing how to navigate it. This complaint seems frivolous in the face of losses among my friends and relatives. They have suffered in ways that I cannot imagine. My children live, my cancer ceased, I have always had food and shelter, my life looks like a latticework apple pie, soft and sweet in places, crusty and burned in others but ultimately a satisfying experience—until now.

My friends tire of my discontent and wonder if I am depressed. They suggest dating services, perhaps a new car purchase, or a trip somewhere to lift my spirit. My father referring to the inflation of my body wants to know when it will stop. My mother indiscreetly lays diet plans ripped from *Prevention Magazine* near the guest bed in her house and makes an appointment for me to see a clairvoyant. The clairvoyant suggests that I sell my house and wear playful clothes. I do not take any of these suggestions and I do not have any answers. As far as I can see, there is only exhaustion, anguish, misery, grief. And there is surprise. I know that my friends with young children may look at this place in my life with private envy. I know this because I was once that mother of young children yearning for a moment to just be. I remember experiencing a fifteen-minute bathroom sabbatical without interruption like one might experience an adult-only cruise. I am surprised the grief of this transition overlays the joy of getting my secret wish.

With this in mind I try not to flaunt my sorrow. I say that I am fine. I hire a writing coach. I join a gym. I make a list of financial goals. I apply for a job. I try to practice detachment. I am detached from myself. Every interaction seems to be in code. My jeans are tighter. Everyone has stopped calling. I can't feel anything anymore. I want to scream at myself, "You fucking drama queen!" And right when I think that my head will explode, it doesn't. But my heart does. I get quiet about my pain. My friends and family think I am over my ridiculous sadness and I begin to cry. I cry anytime that I am not on duty to some person. I cry especially in traffic until I feel that it is a safety hazard. I cry so hard and so often that when I glance out my window, passengers in nearby cars will give me a thumbs-up sign or wave in what feels like some kind of understanding. I park my car in my driveway and cry until bedtime, my neighbors trying not to glance my way, possibly embarrassed for me. I cry in my therapist's office until she says that watching me is beginning to be painful. I cry after a phone conversation. I cry when I write a birthday card to my niece. I cry.

I cry for twelve months and then I suddenly stop. My house really, really, really is empty. I do not have to make nice with classmate's parents or a mother-in-law or be home at a certain time or keep food in my house. I can make plans without considering anyone else. I move my piano into my dining room and contemplate learning how to play. I paint another wall lime green. I realize that my life has changed and I with it. This external thing has happened: My husbands have left and my children have grown into adults triggering a shift that feels like a subdermal injury that you can't see from the surface but causes a great tear, perhaps of the fascia, accompanied by internal bleeding. And right when I think I am going to lie down and bleed out, I don't.

I am beginning to sleep through the night and eat leafy greens again. I sometimes go kayaking in the dark, leaning back to watch the stars, drifting, peaceful. Last week I climbed to the top of Enchanted Rock and took a nap near a shallow indention filled with water and when I awakened, a sparrow, less than a foot from my face, stopped her bathing in the water and smiled at me. I spent a morning stalking redfish with my brother, floating over the oyster reefs, smiling while he paddled. I visit with my sister by phone and feel supported and loved. My grandson has learned to throw a tantrum and to give kisses. I get it. Time has passed.

DONNALYN WATT, A BORN storyteller, has worked as a restaurant owner, counselor, and textile artist. She writes from her home in Dripping Springs, Texas, where she lives with her dog Sophie, a piano, and ceramic flamingos.

Debbie Lee Wesselmann

Before Loss

MY BROTHER AND I do not speak as often as we should: We reserve phone calls for birthdays and Christmas. As siblings, we keep our distance, not because of any dislike or tension, but rather out of habit. My sister and I may talk several times a week, sometimes even several times a day, but my interaction with my brother is more infrequent. This past May, I called him on his birthday, spoke about his life and mine, his family and my family, then closed with an, "I'll see you soon," since we planned to spend an extended family vacation together in less than a month. When he called again two weeks later, I knew something was wrong. The phone calls were too close together and the family vacation was only a week away. Before the tones of his "Hello, Debbie" had faded, my thoughts had already raced to our parents, both in their seventies. When he then said he had received a call from one of our cousins, I felt enormous relief, then the thudding fear that something had happened to my uncle, maybe my aunt. Instead, however, my brother delivered the news with his characteristic monotone delivery: Our 36-year-old cousin Todd, the baby of our generation, had been found dead in his apartment, the victim of an undiagnosed congenital heart defect.

I never knew Todd well. My father and my uncle kept in touch only loosely, through their wives, and even that communication had been spotty over the years. Still, I have a vivid mental picture of Todd gleaned from the first time I met him. He was a toothy toddler with a goofy grin, wearing a huge rainbow button pinned to his shirt, riding his tricycle. He was so exuberantly three-years old that he imprinted himself, fixed exactly this way—even years later—on my memory. I did not see him again until he was ten or so, and then, for a brief period, every year as he matured into a teenager. Again, our families let months become years. I never knew Todd as an independent adult, so why then, as the shock wore off, did I feel such difficult grief? The easy answer to this question is: "Because he died so young, with so much of his life ahead of him," but I know that is not the truth. A person does not feel grief at lost potential; a person grieves because of loss.

Many of my friends have recently lost their parents. You reach a certain age and this inevitability starts to tug at your psyche. You wake up feeling old yourself, and then your mind goes to your parents. They seem vulnerable, fragile, even if they are in excellent health. As others mourn, you cannot help thinking that you will be next and you hope to God that you are not.

The grief of others makes me look at my parents and wonder how much more time I have with them. If genetics are any indication, I have at least a decade, maybe longer, as their child. But I don't know this. As I watch my father step tentatively off a curb or my mother fiddle with a zipper, I have already begun grieving for them. I want them not to be old. I want them—and me—to be still grappling with the vastness of the future, to be powerful and ambitious and agile. So, when I grieve this way in increments, before I actually lose them, I am mourning their youth, what has been lost and what has yet to be lost—what I will miss. I will no longer be able to pick up the phone to share a laugh with my mother or to ask my father for a recipe.

My aunt and uncle never expected to wake up minus one child. Because this end seemed too impossible, the incremental preparation never happened. They expected a more predictable passing of the generations. Everyone did. When we joined together in their home in Ohio, all in shock at the news, they fell back into their expert roles as host and hostess, treating us all like honored guests by fixing dinner and pouring wine and arranging flowers as the centerpiece of their dining room table. They did not know what to do. My uncle looked at my aunt and said, "You have to tell me how to do this. I don't know how to grieve." As though mourning were something that had a manual, a procedure that could be neatly outlined and followed—as though burying your child could be somehow gotten over.

During the two days before the memorial service, people from outside the family offered stories of my cousin's life. My aunt and uncle met with his co-workers and friends to try to piece together Todd's life as a means of holding onto him. And what they heard surprised them. Their son, quiet and gentle and always smiling, had been more than that: He had lived beyond their reach. They learned of his charity work, his way of motivating co-workers, the deep love others felt for him—details he had never shared with them. He was their reserved child. To others, he was the bedrock of their group, the one everyone could turn to and count on. Although this revelation of who Todd really was seemed to warm my aunt and uncle, I could not help thinking that they must have also felt deeper grief because of it: They had not fully known their own son.

Children, however, are like that. Once they go off to kindergarten, parental knowledge and power shifts as the outside world makes its first meaningful intrusion into a child's development. As our children grow older, we are separated from them, stage by stage: the social angst of pre-adolescence, the private lives of teenagers, the distant experiences of college students, the compartmentalization of the working world, and, finally, the largest break, marriage and the deep love they have for what to us is a stranger. Mothers burst into tears as their five-year-olds march off to their first day of school, just as they cry at their adult children's weddings. These are always bittersweet losses because they are neither sorrowful nor final.

Although it seems rudimentary to say, the finality of death is the source of all grief. There will be no more chapters, no more transitions, no more opportunities to fix what is wrong, no more future. The acute stab of this knowledge releases that guttural bellow of mourning. So it was with my mourning for Todd. I did not know him well and now I had no chance to change it. I had no defining adult moment with him, as one of his other cousins did, to replace the toothy three-year-old image. Instead, I knew him by family grapevine, news passed along the phone lines that supplied details but never personality. Except for one. When Todd was a teenager, I asked my aunt about him. She told me that Todd had been diagnosed with a severe learning disability. I'll never forget what she said next: "I've had to change what I want for Todd. I only hope that someday he will be able to live on his own." I wanted to cry then, for her and for Todd, since the future seemed suddenly limited and small for both. However, Todd not only learned to function despite his disability, but he also graduated from college, secured a good job, gained a host of loyal friends, and spread goodwill to strangers. He made the most of the short life he was given. But I did not know this until it was too late. Over the years, I had remained a stranger to him except at weddings and funerals. This was my grief: I had had a wonderful cousin who I had loved, even distantly, but who I never really knew. I mourned not only for him, but for my aunt and uncle who had to bury him, and for my cousins, his brothers, who had perhaps taken him a little for granted as well.

Because of Todd's death, I have tried to be more forgiving toward my parents, more patient. I want both to protect them and to know the details of their day-to-day lives. Although I may be grieving for them in increments, I also realize that they may instead have to grieve one day for me, and so I try to share more about myself. I don't want them, or me, to mourn in regret. Death is powerful enough without having to learn that you did not know someone as much as you should have. For that reason, I am going to call my brother. His heart will stutter when he hears my voice and he will think at once that something has happened to one of our parents. In the end, however, he will rejoice that my call bears no bad news, that I only want to hear what he and his family are doing.

❧ ❧ ❧

DEBBIE LEE WESSELMANN IS the author of two novels, *Captivity* and *Trutor & the Balloonist*, and a collection of short fiction, *The Earth and the Sky*. She has received a New Jersey State Council on the Arts Fellowship and several awards for her short fiction. A graduate of Dartmouth College and Fairleigh Dickinson University, she currently lives in Pennsylvania, where she teaches English at Lehigh University.

Holly Whittaker

A Story of Grief

Two years have dragged by
In big heavy boots
Impossible to lift from the weight of sorrow soaking them
Yet, dragged me they have
And left me, shaking in the moonlight
To fold
Or
Hope.

9/22/05

"HEY, MOMMASITA!" MY DAUGHTER Kerri is on the phone. It is a bright, beautiful morning. The sunlight pouring through the backyard trees of our "new" house creates a golden, sacred light. This is the new family home, though only my youngest child Austin still lives with me. This house is really ours, following years of rental houses. Austin was ecstatic when we moved in—*his* room, alone. He sawed off and discarded unwanted bits and nailed his broken skateboards to his walls and otherwise devalued the house with great joy. Here he comes now, skimming down the hall, sailing through the kitchen. That boy is always in motion, always smiling. He kisses me goodbye as

Kerri wishes me a safe and happy trip to Big Bend. My fiftieth birthday is in three days and I am retreating to the desert to climb my favorite mountain there. Kerri is claiming it's to prove I'm "on top" of the hill, rather than "over" the hill. That girl is a smarty-pants! No respect! Austin's off to catch the city bus to school. I won't drive him as I usually do, as I want to get on the road soon. He hugs my head, kissing my crown. This is his new embrace. Now that he's sixteen and suddenly tall, he likes to make a production of bending over to kiss his "little Mommy" on the head. "Goodbye, my Angel," I call after him. He's leaving early I see. Probably due to the grief I gave him for being late the other day.

We all suffer from grief in our lives. No one escapes tears. Somehow, we must make our way through the quagmire of hope and loss. In my life, I have suffered and cried in the night for relief that never comes. I can count the worst: the brutal tragedy of my first marriage; my baby lost to miscarriage when little Austin was two; having to leave my husband, whom I loved so much; the suffering and death of my beautiful mother; the loss of friends through death or darkness of mind. Life is hard and beautiful, giving joy and love and snatching them away.

I have cried and struggled to find my way through a life that was hard and so often cruel. And I won with love. Love and the needs of my children kept me hopeful and resilient. As a mother, I had no choice but to continue capturing tatters of joy and weaving them into hope for my children's dreams to feed on. And we had such fun: My daughter Kerri, who is the joy born from the ruins of my first dreadful marriage, was nine when charming, smiling Zachary was born of my second marriage and thirteen when Austin followed to bless us with his quiet, strong ways. She was their other mother. The four of us were close and very happy. We had no money. It was difficult and needs were redefined daily. But we enjoyed life together as a great adventure. We sacrificed for each other when needed, celebrated our triumphs, and just had so much fun. When Kerri returned home at age twenty-five to bear Gavin, our little family was complete. Austin, who was then thirteen, was entranced with our sweet baby boy. He spent hours playing with him and cared for him every day—for free, uncomplaining, so that Kerri could go back to college.

I continue to skirt the subject here. It is still so impossible. How to accept the unacceptable? How do you live when life has nothing but pain to offer? Pain is not the word. There are no words. Though people bring them by the bushel loads. Everyone offers up their rationalizations, their excuses, their vision of heaven, and their empty words. I think they are trying to help, but whether it is me or themselves they seek to comfort, I cannot tell. They best keep their mouths shut and hug me.

Zachary lies curled into a ball in the front yard. He cannot stand. He cannot talk. He sobs incoherently, unaware of the world around him. He cannot enter the house. He cannot look at Austin's friends and their parents, who have gathered here wordlessly. I didn't know what to do when they began to appear. "What are you doing here?" I wonder. "Austin isn't here. I can't help you." But they came and they stayed. He has such good friends. We do. We are so very blessed with love.

I lie awake at night, my hand stretched out beside me, clasping his hand. I talk to him all night long. A mockingbird sings outside in the night. Night after night, the mockingbird sings her many and varied songs while I clasp my dead son's hand and talk to him. I know he is scared. That he misses me. Misses his strong active body. Misses this life he embraced so completely. He had so much fun, enjoyed everyone, everything. Austin was the cuddliest of my children. Putting him to bed at night took time. Every night he would invent new series of kisses: "First the regular kiss, Mom, then a butterfly kiss on each cheek, then an Eskimo kiss, now two more regular kisses on the forehead, then two hugs, and then…. No, Mom, you messed up. You have to start again!" In my other hand, I cradle Squirrelly, his favorite stuffed animal. A couple of weeks ago, Austin resurrected Squirrelly from somewhere. I was going to tease him about this battered old stuffed animal in his cool, hip, teenage room. Now I know that Squirrelly is here to comfort me. I hold Austin's hand and try to comfort him, to love him, to comfort myself. I tell him that he is still with me and always will be. Nothing can break this love. With my other hand I clasp Squirrelly to me, his fur matted with all the sweat and grime that Austin's little hands hugged into him over all the years.

The mockingbird comes to my bedroom window by day and hangs on the thin metal strip, peering inside. And I shout at it. "What the hell are you?" "What are you doing here?" "What do you mean?" These are the words I hold in when well-meaning people offer me their carefully constructed rationalizations, their well-intentioned words. I do not want to offend them or burst their carefully constructed glass houses. I, too, have sought to comfort people on occasion, have tried to offer consolation or hope. But we are all deluded. We have not one clue. Austin has taught me the lesson well. Life is a mystery. No one knows why life happens as it does. Our minds try, but can only fail. God has a plan, my ass. Maybe your god, in your little head can rationalize killing Austin. Spare me your attempts, please.

Two days before he was killed, Austin told Kayla, "If anything ever happens to me, you know, like an accident or anything, I wouldn't want anyone to cry. I want everyone to have a big old party." This is real. How could he know? Life is a mystery. I cannot hope to understand.

We did celebrate. I talked about his life, how full of life and joy he was. Everyone told "Austin stories." There are so many: stories of his big heart and silliness and loyalty to friends. His running, jumping, hugging body was cremated that day as the chapel overflowed and people stood in droves outside in the heat to honor this best of boys. At the close, we cheered our boy. No moment of silence for my outrageous-living son. We celebrated the love he engendered in this world. We tried not to cry, Angel Boy.

I cry and scream and tear my hair. Over and over. It does not get any easier to bear. It is so odd how our brains work, finding reasons again and again why it cannot be true. Even recently, moving his couch for the first time, I realized I was holding my breath in anticipation. That under the couch might be some hidden communication, some talisman that would negate the nightmare. Nights I continue to weep and hold Austin's hand and clutch Squirrelly to me. The mockingbird has taken its song and fled. Whether from my continued railing at it or due to Austin's cat on the roof eying its perch outside my window, I don't know. Daytimes I am in a daze, wandering my house, picking up nonexistent lint, crying. Stephanie or Kerri collects me and carts me around in some semblance of life. I worry for Zachary. His friends say he is drinking too much. He drops out of college. I drop out of work. Kerri is held together by her role as a mother. She has to keep Gavin and herself in school, make dinner, be a good mom. She still has so much unresolved grief. While Zach and I howl ours to the moon, destroy and remake ourselves over and over again, Kerri just keeps on, each day. We all fear for Gavin. Aut and "the Kid" were inseparable, and he is only four-years old. How do we discuss death? But Gavin is unperturbed. He comforts his mother a few days after as she cries, "Don't be sad, Mom. Aut told me last night that he's having more fun flying up there." We are awestruck. That is exactly what Austin would say! He found such joy in everything. What does it mean? We don't press Gavin. A month after Austin is killed, Gavin says, "Grandma, I think Aut should come back now." Oh, baby boy, death does not work like that. And now, just two weeks ago, Gavin finally broke down and howled hot bitter tears over losing his Aut. He is six now and understands so much more. He realizes what he has lost.

I discover depression and anxiety. I am completely debilitated. My physical body breaks down, every former injury returning to haunt me like an old familiar friend. I can't get up. Any demand completely undoes me. I can't do it—anything. And my mind can say, as my friends do, "Oh, but you have so much to live for!" Depression does not actually respond to rationale. Every day to wake up and realize again that the sweetest boy is gone. How to accept the unacceptable? I do refuse to accept it. Acceptance implies that it is all right.

One day, writing in my journal, I see my hand write, "Austin has been the only sadness in my life." Oh, my god! How could I say that? Think that? My boy has been only joy to the entire world. I realized then that somehow I needed to reclaim the joy of Austin. I could not let his being killed destroy me or diminish the love and joy he brought to this dark world.

It is not easy. Listen to the words: "Get over it." That will never happen. "Accept it." Where do we get these concepts? These stupid words? And now it's been two long years. Every morning when I wake up, my sweet boy is still dead. I have to make my own coffee. He will never proudly bring me coffee again or care for me when I am ill, beat me every cribbage game, or follow me, off trail and hidden, while we hike together.

There is something about such a catastrophic event that can remove our "civilized view" of the world. In the time after Austin was killed, I saw connections, unimaginable beauty in wretched pain. Daily rationality fell away and revealed a world united only by thin wisps of love, which floated freely yet wove endless beauty. We have no word but magic to describe the way events and circumstances come together and fall apart. This complicated world, which we believe we own and understand, is only so much lint in our brain. We think we understand because we are fed explanations all our lives. But explanations are only words, and they fail in the face of the mystery.

Austin broke my world and is teaching me now to live with the mystery we call life. So I learn to live day to day, moment to moment, to be open to new opportunities and experiences, to trust my heart and accept the beautiful gifts of this world. Learn to live with the pain of life. Great teachers also have come to me in this broken time and helped my heart. They each have affirmed the mystery that I realized when Austin was killed.

My grandson, Gavin—it is impossible to cry when he is insisting on turning over every rock in my yard in his determined search for worms. He will not let me off—every rock must be inspected. We find no worms, but lots of really gross looking bugs, and I do not die of grief that day. Gavin and I use each other to fill the void of Aut in our lives. He telephones me, "Grandma, Mom's being boring. Let's go hiking." We feel Austin with us, when Gavin catches his first fish with his hands, just as Aut used to. When he jumped off the top of McKinney Falls recently, I saw Aut in the spray. Laughing his head off at the Kid's nerve and heart, so like his mentor.

In this mystery, Austin comes to me in dreams. He lets me know that he is all right and encourages me to grow and be well. The mockingbird wakes me singing when these dreams come, so I can be aware of them. The mockingbird? But she's been gone all these months! A mystery. There was the dream in which Austin was a dragonfly and couldn't live in my house… and then the (undreamed, real, live) dragonfly that came in the middle of the night, as I read on the porch, sleepless. Large and green, just like in the dream, he hurled himself relentlessly, over and over against my screen door, until I said that I would be all right, that I would survive. At which point, the dragonfly lifted up off the floor to which he'd fallen after his last suicidal crash against the door and flew off over my roof. Dragonflies are not nocturnal. Their species rests at night, and I have no body of water nearby to house one.

This life cannot be explained or justified. It simply is. I try to stay away from dashed expectations, such as what a great father Austin would have been and how I would have loved being grandmother to his children. I rejoice instead in the gifts that he gave us: his unconditional love and joy, his daring and courage, his large circle of friends who continue to celebrate him with us. It is hard to see his pals, all of them eighteen now, bigger, the boys growing mustaches and beards, graduating and moving forward in their lives. It is a blessing to know that each of them continues to honor Austin and his influence in their lives. I try to stay in a state of gratitude for my many gifts, one of which is my youngest son's life. Austin will always be 16, always be my baby boy and greatest teacher.

Austin Weirup was killed by a cement truck driver who "never saw him" before turning into and killing him instantly, five minutes after he kissed his mother on September 22, 2005.

Holly Whittaker was recently relieved of her job and is trying to remember what she wants to be when she grows up. Zach is back at UT; Kerri graduates from St. Edwards University in two weeks. Gavin is the best reader in first grade.

HOLLY WHITTAKER WAS BORN and raised in the Catskill Mountains of upstate New York. There she wandered solitary in fields and forests and wrote poetry for the birds. She abandoned her college studies in art to become a single mother. In 1979, she and her three-year-old daughter drove off in an old army van looking for adventure. Travel remains her favorite meditation. In the course of feeding her children, she has enjoyed many different careers: from machinist to acupuncture assistant, postal carrier to project manager; and has lived in New York, Texas, California, and Nebraska. Holly currently lives in Austin, Texas. She still writes poetry to the birds.

Spike Gillespie

'Til Grief Do We Part

THE MONTH I FILED for divorce, I also had plans to attend a lot of weddings. Eight actually. Not the best time to be repeatedly toasting celebrations of the very institution that ultimately left me reeling, barely able to get out of bed, and saying goodbye to twenty pounds in five weeks. But making last minute excuses not to attend these affairs was not an option. As a wedding officiant, I'm more obligated than a postal worker. Rain, snow, sleet, hail, a pummeled heart—none of these things can stop me from showing up. Without me, there is no wedding.

Besides, I needed the money these gigs paid more than ever. I needed to pay for my divorce. I needed to cover the increased expenses of not splitting the bills anymore. And I needed to save for expensive laser removal and future cover up of the enormous tattoo that prominently featured my ex-husband's name.

The actual ceremonies weren't too bad, once I got going. The times I did get choked up and started crying a little, I like to think were perceived as tears of joy wept for the couple, not grief over my own uncoupling. A slightly weepy officiant is a good thing, giving the distinct impression the preacher is fully present, not just going through the motions.

And the truth is that I remained happy for all the couples I united that month. I admired their hope. I enjoyed their smiles. I loved the spontaneous moments when they clutched each other or the congregation burst out in joyous laughter and wild applause. Often, these moments provided brief flashes of relief for the pain that otherwise tore through me every waking hour.

The hard part, though, was always the drive *to* the wedding. My ex-husband, before he left me, used to go with me. For us these were romantic dates, and a sense that we were renewing our own vows filled us. We ate well, surfed the happy energy abundant at the reception, and fell in love all over again every time.

Three days before I filed, I performed, for the second time, the wedding of a young couple. This was actually just a formal celebration of their first marriage—performed for insurance purposes months in advance of the big soiree. That ceremony was tiny, held on a brisk autumn night at a little chapel down a country road. As we turned off the main highway it dawned on me that I'd been here before.

The preceding spring, to mark her eleventh anniversary, I'd gone with my husband and his kids down this very road, to the place where his last wife's ashes had been scattered. I was honored to have been invited, unsure when the day began if they felt I belonged there with them.

Looking back, I realize that was the feeling I had most of the time I was with them—a feeling that intensified as time wore on and the kids grew increasingly resentful of my presence. I had thought, when I moved in, that it was a lovely way to remember her—all the portraits of her hanging on the walls, her ashes in the spice rack, her possessions scattered throughout the house. But when it became clear that I was not "allowed" to move any of these things, nor was I "allowed" to keep my possessions anywhere but our tiny bedroom, I realized that something was very wrong.

Once, I put a magnet with a picture of my son on the refrigerator. It was soon, without explanation, replaced by a magnet featuring my predecessor. The stack of wedding gifts we left in the living room when we headed out on our honeymoon was shoved into a disorganized heap in our room while we were gone.

Subtle digs gave way to blatant attempts to show me I was not welcome. One night, while I was out, one of the kids smashed all my potted plants and methodically went through the kitchen breaking only my dishes and a few wedding gifts that had crept out of my designated holding pen. The dead wife's sister held holiday dinners insisting my husband attend but banning me from the events.

I finally moved out, but did not give up. The plan was that I would share custody of my husband with his kids who, though legally adults, clearly still did not know how to act grown up. But separate households were never part of my vision of marriage. I grew cranky. Soon, our limited time together involved having the same argument over and over. Me: "You don't give me enough time." Him: "I'll never be able to give you what you need."

I should have seen his departure coming, but I did not. When he announced one night that I could have several months of no contact or a flat out divorce I felt like he'd hit me in the head with a shovel. I could not abide by either choice and the economics of the situation—supply now diminished to no time together whatsoever—sent my addictive impulses into overdrive. I begged. I pleaded. I cried. I yelled. I became so thoroughly unattractive that *I* did not even want to be around me, so it wasn't much of a stretch to see why he didn't either.

If you asked my husband to name the top reasons he left, I think he'd say I was too angry and that he felt I was making him choose between the kids and me. I, of course, would disagree.

My take would be that he and his kids never grieved the last wife, never let her go. As in Joan Didion's *The Year of Magical Thinking*, they kept her things, convinced she would one day come back and need them. When I showed up and slept in "her" bed and used "her" space, that left no space for her return. How weary I grew of listening to tales of this saint, how she never did anything wrong. I knew her birthday, death day, and wedding anniversary. I even knew what she wore the day she married my husband, eighteen years before he became my husband.

They got married in Vegas. She was eight months pregnant, bursting and glowing in her saffron dress. Bursting and glowing like the saffron harvest moon that hung full, heavy and, I couldn't help thinking, very pregnant as it slowly rose in the sky that night we drove down the road, past her ashes, on our way to that little wedding. I instantly thought of her at the sight of it. I imagined her saying: *Appreciate him; let the anger go; be glad you're alive to be married to him because I wish I was.*

At the big wedding of the couple whose small wedding brought me this poetry of full moon and scattered ashes, my husband called right before the ceremony to say he wasn't coming. (I had suggested we use this wedding as closure, since I'd informed him I was divorcing him, but had some absurd hope we could have one last wedding date, try to lay it down gently.)

Though his call didn't surprise me—I was accustomed to him not showing up by then—still I was rattled. I put in a call to my therapist who talked me down. I pulled myself together and joined the procession. I read a passage I was not looking forward to. But they had hired me long ago, and I had not yet removed these words from the *Wedding Ceremony Menu Options*. An excerpt:

Shortly after I met my husband he presented me with a cardboard puzzle piece he found on the ground. He said, "You're my perfect little puzzle piece, you fit just right into my life." It was the best gift I'd ever been given and later we had it cast in silver. I wear it always as a reminder of how fortunate we are to find the people with whom we best fit in this world.

I didn't tell the couple he wasn't there because he'd left me. I just said he had an emergency that kept him away. Upon the insistence of a friend, however, I did inform the following week's couple—who had also chosen this passage—of my circumstances. I asked if we could trade out for something more authentic. They were compassionate but insistent. They loved the story. Would I please keep it in? I did and, because I did, I was forced to get out that necklace and wear it one last time.

At that reception I was approached by a number of people who praised the story. Of my absent husband, one woman said, "He's a real keeper. I had one of those, too, but he died." Another guest wanted to touch the puzzle piece. "Touch it?" I wanted to say. "You can *have* it."

Recently I performed another wedding at that little chapel down the country road. The sky was still light as I drove by the place where her ashes were scattered. I started to cry. I collected myself. I did not call my therapist. I performed the wedding. I got a little weepy. I didn't say why. For reasons I will never understand but forever appreciate, the post-ceremony song was Gloria Gaynor's disco breakup anthem, *I Will Survive.*

Heading home, I pulled over by the little stream and got out of my car and stood watching the water. A rancher type in a pickup pulled over.

"You broke down?" he asked.

"No," I lied.

I spoke to her then. Out loud. Me on a gray spring evening, a chill in the air, the water running fast from recent hard rains. *Please*, I said, *help them let you go. Not for me. It's too late for me. But they are stuck. They won't be happy until they say goodbye.*

Months later, I ran into my ex-stepdaughter unexpectedly. We said hello and exchanged a few words. That night, though the daily tears that flooded me every day all day for the first six months after my ex-husband walked had finally ceased, I found myself again sobbing uncontrollably. I had seen in that young woman's eyes that it was still there—all the grief that had pulled me toward her when we first met. All the grief that triggered an anger in her so deep that she eventually pushed me away in a violent rage. All that unprocessed grief, a grief that haunted her father, too.

A grief I caught, like some airborne illness, that filled me and rattled me and changed me forever.

SPIKE GILLESPIE IS A journalist, author, blogger, knitter, and wedding officiant in Austin, Texas. Her work has appeared in *The New York Times Magazine*, *The New York Times*, *National Geographic Traveler*, *GQ*, *Playboy*, and many other publications. Online her work has been published lots of places, too. Her blog resides at: *spikeg.com*. Her books include *All the Wrong Men and One Perfect Boy*; *Surrender: But Don't Give Yourself Away*; *Pissed Off: On Women and Anger*; and *Quilty as Charged*. She shares her life with her son, Henry; her partner, Ori; and four out-of-control dogs.

Victoria Sullivan Hendricks

And Both Are True

Kerry, my love,

JOANNA TURNED THIRTY LAST *week, and you've been dead twenty-one years. We were twenty-one the year you proposed. The day you turned thirty seems as clear as yesterday. Joanna was almost three, and we'd just found out I was pregnant with Ruth. Joanna helped me frost your chocolate birthday cake, which means she mostly frosted herself. She and I carefully stuck all thirty bright-colored candles into the uneven frosting, and I added "one to dream on." I knew the day was precious, but I didn't know, couldn't imagine, you'd only have five more birthdays.*

We lived in what the kids call "the pink bubble" in those days. We were one of those couples, one of those families people didn't quite believe could be as happy as we looked. I think we really were. We had our delightful growing girl, our baby on the way, our little house in the neighborhood where you'd always wanted to live, grad school underway for both of us, sufficient income. And we still never ran out of things we were dying to say to each other, still couldn't keep our hands off each other. I remember lying in bed one morning that summer, queasy with pregnancy, but happy. You cradled me in one arm and Joanna in the other and mused that it didn't seem fair we had it so easy.

In the hospital waiting room on the Monday before Thanksgiving the year Ruth was four, the pink bubble burst. The surgeon, who had known you since childhood, had tears in his eyes when he told me they'd been wrong. It wasn't a treatable infected cyst in your chest. It was an inoperable tumor. You had a year at most, he said. He gave me an oncologist's address and an appointment time and asked me if I wanted him to tell you the news. But I had to tell you. I would have wanted you to be the one to tell me news like that.

I had to tell you in just a few minutes when you woke from anesthesia. I had to find the strength and words. Even as I stood stunned and apparently calm, taking notes, saying the right words to the doctor, the first wave of grief hit me. It felt like rage. As soon as the doctor left, or maybe without waiting for him to leave, I ran for the nearest, blessedly empty, bathroom. A stack of toilet paper rolls stood against a mirror. I started at the top, grabbed each one and hurled it at the wall until I stood in a mass of strewn rolls. I don't remember if I screamed or cursed, but tears must have flowed because after I'd re-stacked the toilet paper, I looked in the mirror and my face was tear streaked. I do remember running the water, washing my face, even applying the lipstick that I was surprised to find in my purse. I remember telling myself I'd had my fit and now it was time to do what had to be done. Did you notice the lipstick when I told you that you had cancer? Did I seem too calm to you?

I know I seemed too calm to everyone else during the terrible nine months you were sick. But I wasn't calm. Did you know how scared I was? I think I hid it pretty well, even from myself. I had established my pattern for handling the waves of grief in that hospital bathroom. The day I learned the cancer was in your kidneys, I threw canned food in our kitchen. Then I picked it up and cooked dinner. All spring as you struggled with more and more pain I threw rocks in the garden, and then came in and patiently helped Joanna with homework and played games with Ruth. Even the night you died, I got myself home from the hospital and cleaned the house fiercely, then methodically started making lists about how the funeral should be. I raged and then I coped.

We told the girls you were very sick and might die. We used the word cancer. But we used it calmly, without the feeling. At least I did. Did my apparent lack of feeling bother you? It was the best I could do. I couldn't let myself know how much your death would turn our lives inside out, would shatter life as I knew it. I could tell the girls facts, but couldn't let myself accept the meaning of those facts.

Our friends and families, grieving hard themselves and right there with us and for us in every way, kept waiting for me to cry or ask for comfort. I didn't. I couldn't. People may have thought I was cold, but they told me I was strong. I wasn't strong, just terrified. Admitting I needed help would have made the fact that I was going to lose you too real. I wasn't ready for it to be that real.

You were the only one who ever knew how scared I was, and I don't think even you knew until very near the end. The afternoon you went into the hospital the last time, I think we both knew you weren't going to live much longer. I stormed into the bedroom and screamed at you, "Don't you dare die! I can't live without you!" You still had enough lucidity and strength to grab me by the shoulders and compel my gaze with your fire blue eyes. "Yes, you can. And if you have to, you will and you'll do a damn good job of it." It sounded like an order then. I didn't realize until years later that, in that moment, you gave me your blessing to thrive again.

I give lectures about grief now. I run grief groups and counsel others trying to survive their losses. I tell them that grief is the normal process through which people make sense of losses. It is the process of finding a way to survive them. Recovery from grief is the process of allowing ourselves to find a way to thrive again, even though our world will never be the same. Recovery, like grief, comes in waves.

I didn't know anything about the process of grief and recovery twenty-one years ago when I was planning your funeral with our children. I didn't know while I was trying to maintain Girl Scouts and some semblance of normalcy for a nine-year-old who had been her Daddy's princess. I didn't know as I readied a fatherless kindergartner for the first day of school or when I was trying to start a business. All I thought I knew then was that I had no desire to be alive without you. But I had no choice because I had two kids to raise. I lived breath by breath, one foot in front of the other, not feeling much, just doing what I had to do.

There was one moment in October, three months after you died, when I was working in the garage. The first norther of the season blew in, blessing me with that indefinable scent of fall, and I felt happy for an instant. I remember being surprised. I hadn't expected to ever feel happy again. That was the first tiny wave of recovery.

That first year, I mostly just went through the motions, more or less effectively, but without feeling. Our friends kept me company and worried, expecting tears that didn't come that year. I kept myself moving because of the girls' needs and because I could anchor myself in the life you and I had lived. Every day, every action, I framed in terms of "this time last year we…" And that got me through. I was still living my life defined by the life you and I had built together. I couldn't see you or touch you, but you were my anchor and that was enough.

Then the first anniversary of your death came and I couldn't say, "This time last year we" anymore. Friends pushed me to spend the anniversary of your death at a retreat for people grieving marriages, ended either by death or divorce. Even there I went through the motions. I listened to the lectures each with recorded mood music, did the required journaling, and participated in the discussions, but calmly, without much feeling, without tears.

I was a little bored, ready to go home, when I walked into the room for the last lecture and heard the speakers blaring out, "I want to be free." The words hit me like an assault, expressing the possibility I feared most. Wanting to be free would be a step in leaving you behind. I most emphatically did not want to be free. I wanted to be yours, forever. I wouldn't let death change that. The tears poured from the first impact of those words on my brain, hot, wet, noisy, sobbing tears, a toddler's "Don't leave me! I can't live without you!" tears.

I don't remember a word of that lecture or how I managed to stumble out to a bench with my blue notebook to journal. I poured out feelings I hadn't yet given words. "I don't want to be free. I don't want to live without you. I don't want to become a woman you wouldn't recognize, to become someone you don't know. I don't want to change. I don't want to make decisions without bouncing them off you. I don't want to taste meals you'll never taste, read books you'll never read, see movies you'll never see." My entry was repetitive, redundant, tear-splattered. I didn't allow myself to read it for months. I was too frightened.

It wasn't the truth of the words I'd written that scared me, but the fact that as soon as I wrote them they started becoming less true. Would you ever forgive me if I did actually want to be free? Part of me was lonely, wanted change, wanted to date, wanted to be held again, even to be married again. And I hated that part of myself. I felt disloyal, even though, in that last hospital room you told me that you hoped being married to you was good enough to encourage me to look for marriage again.

I felt disloyal, and I wasn't very good at living without you. I spent too much money and worked too much. I didn't talk enough about you to the girls and didn't listen well enough when they talked about their lives. I didn't sleep, cooked potato soup in the middle of the night and ate the whole pot. I didn't try hard enough to find a way to get close to your parents and brothers again. It took me until the second anniversary of your death to get your ashes out of the closet and bury them with a ceremony and build you a marker.

But in the third year, afraid and confused as I was, I let myself fall in love again. Before the third anniversary of your death, Bob and I married. I made that choice too fast, didn't give the girls enough time to warm up to the changes involved in being a family with someone who wasn't you. I didn't give myself enough time.

I got mad at Bob when he showed me that he wasn't you, even in trivial ways, like wanting ketchup on his hamburger or having a sense of direction, which you didn't have at all. It wasn't easy and I was still grieving you harder than I wanted to admit. I was trying to recreate the pink bubble and that wasn't going to happen. Your death had blown that bubble apart, not just cracked it. Remarriage was as useless as superglue.

Bob and I and the girls had to build something completely new from scratch. I should have known that, but I didn't. Every time I tried to re-create something you and I had done, a way we'd been together, it felt hollow and wrong, and I just missed you more. I hurt everyone around me, and I didn't seem to be able to live in the present, without referencing back in my heart to our life together and to what life would have been like if you'd lived. Through my misguided efforts to re-create our past, I came closer than I want to know to ruining a real chance to build a strong marriage and family with Bob.

But Bob is as good a man as you were, and he was patient with me and the girls. He also was strong enough to keep on being himself. He didn't give in to my efforts to mold him into the image of the man I believed you would have become. We fought. I said mean things. I saw the hurt in his eyes, and I saw the love, too, and little by little, he and I have built a marriage that is about us, not about you and me.

I'm happy. Most people I meet now don't know I was widowed young. I know though. I will always be defined in part by having been loved by you and by having lost you. We grew into adulthood together, finished college, bought our first house, had babies, and created our images of who we wanted to be in the world together. I will always miss you. Every time I look at our children, at grandchildren with your eyes, I see you and wonder how it would have been if you'd lived. Every time I see an elderly couple walking unsteadily in our neighborhood at sunset, I remember the evening you pointed out such a couple, squeezed my hand and said, "Someday that will be us."

I still cry that we didn't get that someday. And I am happy with the days I have now. Life force does come back. I will always miss you. Both statements are equally true.

Always,
Victoria

VICTORIA SULLIVAN HENDRICKS WORKS as a life coach and takes great satisfaction in abiding with people whose personal worst has happened. She sees herself as an experienced trail guide on the path away from the shards of a previous life through the process of building a transformed life. Every workday she gets more evidence that love and life are stronger than loss. Victoria lives in Austin with her husband and near her daughters and grandchildren.

Miriam Kuznets

Joining the Club

THE OTHER DAY I was talking with friends who remembered being teenagers and reveling in the alternate worlds and meaningful allegories of J.R.R. Tolkien and C.S. Lewis. Not me—I wanted my world straight up. The authors I remember from that time, Judy Blume and S.E. Hinton, may never be in the canon, but back then, they hit the pubescent, nitty-gritty spot: the bloodiness of menstruation, tough peers, scary and sometimes deadly experimentation. These books revealed the noir Charlie Brown world where parental protection is, however benignly intended, distant and incomprehensible. Through literature verité I found, at a safe distance, camaraderie. I found guidance in what I would later see as a life-long quest to survive loss well.

After college I found a job at a literary agency. The agent with whom I worked very closely, Eric Ashworth, became like the big brother I never had. Eric was gay, young, and handsome in a tall, broad-shouldered way. Our desks near enough for us to make eye contact, we talked easily. Though I probably shouldn't have been, I was in charge of the "slush pile," the unsolicited manuscript submissions, and when I found a gem, Eric shared my enthusiasm. John Cheever had been a client of the agency and Eric made me read that masterpiece of shattered illusions,

"The Swimmer." Eric and I smoked cigarettes. We cracked up. We lunched at the local coffee shop on tuna melts and French fries. We sat next to each other, weeping, at "Night, Mother." Eric and his partner Rick took me out to expensive dinners and let me stay in their place when they were out of town. Eric gave me a shoulder to cry on when I found out that a good friend, whose apartment I was subletting and who hadn't paid the rent, was a heroin addict.

My maternal grandmother was another older person who was nicer to me than she had to be. I'd visited her a lot over the years, often arranging to visit my father at her house in Cambridge. Whatever stages I went through—from my almost-black lipstick to my proudly showing her a close-up of my and a college boyfriend's mouths French-kissing—the only thing she criticized about me was my anglicized pronunciation of Nabokov. My grandfather died at around the time I graduated college and after that I visited Grandma even more often. We whiled away many a late afternoon in her living room, sipping sherry and eating smoked almonds. I loved hearing about her life—from the pickle barrel in her father's store in Queenstown, Ontario, to her dancing awkwardly with a short Chinese dignitary on one of my grandfather's business trips in the 1940s.

Around that time, I had an image of life as an infinite colander through which we human drops constantly fall, washing away. If I could help keep others from falling, as well as myself, I would be doing good. Instead of veering away from suffering, I would be turning into the skid. So, I volunteered for a few shifts at the Victim Services Agency's call center. However disembodied, I tried to be understanding and helpful when I spoke to the caller at the other end of the line.

Around that time, I had a couple of stories published—one was about a woman grieving over her ex-boyfriend, one was about a woman grieving her friend's death. I left New York for Iowa to get an MFA in fiction writing.

Back in New York, Eric tested positive for HIV. When Eric told me, I felt as if someone had whacked me in the heart with a club. Eric and his family had already tragically lost Eric's oldest brother to AIDS. The solid, wonderful Eric began his long descent.

After graduating and doing some teaching in freezing upstate New York, I moved to Austin just because it was sunny, not too big, and not too small. Then, since I wasn't going to live near Eric, I wanted to be there for someone with AIDS. I began to volunteer for AIDS Services of Austin. Through the Buddy program, I met Jim, an early thirties-ish, bespectacled, blonde guy who was on disability. We hung out, chatted, and ate turkey sandwiches together. I accompanied him on sunny days to doctor's appointments in windowless offices.

I lacked the drive and talent to be a writer or to do writing-related jobs, and I started to picture how I might make a living for the next forty-odd years. I saw myself sitting and listening to someone; in my mind's eye, I was leaning forward in my chair—not from bad posture but from my effort to connect to the person across from me. I decided that what I wanted to do for a living was therapy. I wanted to provide a safe place for people to open up about what hurt and what helped.

Getting a master's in clinical social work would enable me to be a psychotherapist, so back to grad school. Because I was getting busier, my buddy Jim and I agreed that it was time for him to get a new buddy, though we kept up for a while.

In school, I scoured the journals to see what those who studied grief had to say. The research, in sources with heavy titles like *Omega: The Journal of Death and Dying*, claimed that there was no single healthy way to cope with grief. Some people needed to talk a lot about their loss. Some people didn't. Some people needed to have their loved one's belongings around them. Others needed to give away the closet full of clothes as quickly as possible. Some experienced Kübler-Ross's stages of grief in the neat line that she described, while others skipped Bargaining and went to Depression before Anger, or maybe didn't experience distinct stages at all. I read about the grief burnout in people whose circles were dying from AIDS—how could they mourn one death when another followed close at the heels? Of course, I thought of Eric, his friends, his family.

As part of my internship at a social services agency, I was given the chance to start a group of my choice. I established a bereavement group, which quickly filled with women whose husbands had died. Though at that point, I was unmarried and childless, some collective unconscious, perhaps, made me feel wells of empathy for them. I particularly remember the woman with the coppery hair who had lost her marathon-running husband, the father of her two sons, to leukemia. She cried, she laughed, and she told it like it was.

After graduation, I worked at a psychiatric hospital, which was really more like a psychiatric emergency motel. The patients' grief—over having a mental illness, over losing loved ones through divorce or death, over a mountain of perceived failures—left me overwhelmed. During my two years at the hospital, I was stunned that five of the patients who had been in therapy groups I'd facilitated committed suicide. But this was par for the course. I ruminated and wept over whether I could have done anything to help fuel their will to live; I tried to imagine their desperation. Since my fellow therapists had also worked with these clients, we were sad together. Although I'd quit smoking long before, I started going for smoke breaks with my co-workers and bumming cigarettes.

I was getting depressed myself. My boyfriend at the time was licking his own wounds from a too-recent divorce, and our relationship died, as it should have long before.

I needed to get out of the trenches, so I bought my own house and quit the psych hospital to start working at a clinic. There I started a divorce recovery group. I could identify with the death of relationship dreams, with the sadness of someone being there in such a big way, and then not being there at all. At work, I continued to talk all day with people about their pain. The *aha* moments, the breaking of chains (some self-imposed), the stubborn life force that my clients experienced made the work meaningful.

I saw in the obituaries that my buddy Jim had died; he was still only in his thirties.

I also read an article about widows and widowers in the paper. It made me smile because it featured the coppery-haired woman and the widower she'd met and married. I knew her first husband was still in her heart.

My fellow therapist friend Judy and I attended the film society's Film Noir and Femme Fatale series—a busman's holiday. We joked about how nice it was to not have to do anything about all the suffering and "acting out" these characters did.

Rick, by then Eric's ex-partner but still good friend, called to tell me that Eric had died. I put Eric's picture, a head shot, on the refrigerator, where I knew I'd see it a lot, and in the months that followed, I said silently to him, "Here's looking at you." The three-dimensional, full-length Eric in my memory was always in a gray suit that was particularly becoming.

My ninety-six-year-old grandmother died soon after that. Before she died, I wrote her a long letter, possibly sparked by Eric's death, in which I told her how much she meant to me. After her death, I inherited a lot of places to sit—sofas, chairs—places where she'd sat.

It was a strange world without these two people I'd so delighted in and who, I believe, delighted in me.

I started a private practice and a "Writing to Heal" group. I joined a therapy group myself. I worked on my psyche and my posture. My father had mellowed over the years, as had I. He introduced me to Django Reinhardt, and I was impressed by what dexterity Django had developed after the loss of two fingers.

Despite surrounding myself with the weight of the world, I always had a playful side, which came out most in romantic relationships—as did my not-so-lovely baggage. More years passed, as did more relationships. I found camaraderie in my tried-and-true ways. I also appreciated another form of relief: One day, I was lying on the sofa crying after a breakup. The cat, my petite therapist, was on my chest. I started *Me Talk*

Pretty One Day by David Sedaris, one of the few writers who can make me laugh aloud. Swollen-eyed and snotty-nosed, me not so pretty, I cracked up.

Then, at thirty-eight, serendipity: I found my one-and-only husband Max. He is Mr. Right for Me—witty, kind, playful, solid, with a face I love. I delight in him. Two years later, I gave birth to Max's and my greatest delight, my now four-year-old Eli. Eli is much like his father, though, as befits a youngster, less solid. Eli is much like me in his stubborn persistence. Max is a fabulous, fun father. I'm so grateful for my boys.

Still, last year, was full of grief. My mother found out that she had advanced ovarian cancer. Much pain and suffering later, she's alive and well and acting in local theater. When we didn't know if she'd be around this year, I wept and panicked and started to grieve.

At the same time, I discovered that I too had some senseless bad luck—the genetic mutation that, we now see, has brought so much grief and early death through breast and ovarian cancer to the women on my mother's side. The odds were that I'd get one of these cancers. I could also get hit by a bus. But I and, amazingly, the insurance company decided that prevention was the best cancer cure. I decided to mourn the loss of my female parts—all of them—in order to increase my odds of sticking around a little longer for the party and for my little boy. Hellish surgeries and recoveries later, I have faux boobs and barely any estrogen of my own. But I think I still have my best parts.

Max and I have looked over our wedding photos and have seen that in the five years since we've married, several of the people at the wedding have died—including my mother's sister, of breast cancer; several have divorced; several have gotten married; several have had babies. One of the people who died was Ira Greenspan, of colon cancer at age fifty-two. At his funeral, I remember people honoring him, saying that Ira was someone who always showed up. I thank the people, dead and alive, who've been there for me.

When I was recovering from surgery, but still in pain, my family and friends were enormously helpful. Showing up at work also helped me. In my office, I saw myself and my clients as part of a club of frail yet resilient humans, humans who wanted to get back to seizing the day. And during that healing time, at home, I could only read and watch things that were funny, but still vérité, of course.

❧ ❧ ❧

MIRIAM KUZNETS IS A psychotherapist in Austin, Texas, where she lives with, and is most grateful for, her husband and son. She has an MFA from the Iowa Writers' Workshop. Her work has appeared in various literary magazines and has won awards from *Poets & Writers* magazine and Barnard College. Miriam plans to work on this grief and loss stuff for the rest of her life.

Amy Friedman

New Year's Day

THERE WAS THIS DAY, New Year's Day, difficult enough on any ordinary year—all that pressure to feel vital and newly born—but this particular day was the beginning of the seventh year G and I were married, and it was the start of the year we might actually live together. It was just two months before his parole hearing.

G and I met when he had already served seven years in prison. I was working as a newspaper columnist. I walked into the penitentiary where he lived and we fell in love. That always arouses gasps of disbelief, but there's not much to that part of the story. We fell in love the way people do—nothing all that different from the way I'd fallen in love with other men, even though G was serving thirteen-to-life for murder. He was once a drug dealer; he shot and killed another dealer on a miserable spring morning in a little northern Ontario town. When we married, I understood he wouldn't be eligible for parole, even for day parole, for more than six years, and, no, we didn't make love before we married.

But up until that New Years' Day, for nearly seven years, G and his daughters—teenagers who lived with me—were the center of my life. I knew a lot of people snickered behind my back about our marriage; I saw the disdain or pity on others' faces. I was, after all, a Seven Sisters School graduate, a woman from a wealthy American suburb, well-bred and well-born, and even though lots of women talk about how appealing those boys from the wrong side of the tracks can be and so many of those women think, well, yeah, okay, having sex with them would be okay—behind bushes, under stadium seats, in the dark, in summertime—nearly every one of them also believes, fiercely and firmly, that it's not okay to marry them. I knew a lot of people who thought that.

Still, at first I told everyone about us, and when they asked what he'd done, I'd tell them, murder. Maybe that was the rebel in me, but nobody knew G—and no one except those willing to visit prison could know him—so all I had was our story. So at first I liked to tell it. That's why I know the kinds of questions people have.

Most people wanted to know if he was fabulous looking. Well, he wasn't Robert Redford or Paul Newman or Russell Crowe or any of those movie bad guys with their makeup and great lighting and lots of hip clothing that fits perfectly, but he was a handsome guy, well built though he tended to put on pounds—he was that type—and so he worked it off, became slender and muscular. His hair once was blond, and he thought it still was when we met, but by then, though he was only 38, it had turned silvery grey. He had blue eyes, yes, piercing blue, and he wasn't tall but he wasn't short, and he had a firm handshake, though as I recall our hands were the same size. And when we fell in love I felt the way everyone does—heady, stomach a little empty and turning somersaults whenever he laughed and talked and when we kissed. I remember his lips as soft, and I remember loving his anger, too—because I was angry at the same things he was—man's inhumanity to man, selfishness, unwarranted cruelty. He read a lot. He grew up in a middle class family. He had a doctor sister, a nurse sister, a businesswoman sister. His mom was wonderful. He was an athlete who took a wrong turn—a terrible turn.

The few people who visited prison and met him—Kate, Diane, Anndale, my mom and dad—understood why I loved him. They always remembered that his voice was rich and deep, and so was his laugh. In fact, his laugh was delicious, the kind of infectious laugh you can never forget. Anndale was the first to point that out, and Kate spoke of his eyes with all their sadness and loneliness, and the way they lit up whenever he had visitors.

Okay, so maybe I just liked bringing warmth into a lonely man's life, and maybe the marriage was pure ego, but then, I always thought, every marriage is in some way.

And, yeah, he had his lines. The casually tossed off, "I want my daughters to meet you—my daughters need to meet an impressive woman," but he wasn't the only man who ever used that line on me. Lots of Harvard-educated lawyer-types had used the same line because, face it, it's the kind of line that works on women like me, women who like to think we are professional, that we cannot be conned.

Still, a lot of people thought, and some said out loud, "Oh man, Amy fell for a con," and they said, "Why do you think they call them cons?" and "God, could you ever…you know…could you?" They never asked outright, "Did you ever make love?" But, yes, we did, once every three months in a trailer on the prison grounds, behind walls and gates and under lock and key, and later I found out that guards could listen if they wanted to. I found that out because once one did, and he let me know that as I was leaving prison grounds after one more goodbye.

The fact is, I'd never talked with anyone the way I talked with G. I'd never had that kind of time. Nobody does. Two and three and four and six hours each day, seven days a week for nearly seven years at a table, sharing a bottle of water or a coffee or tea. That was it. Except for those rare trailer visits, we just sat together in sterile rooms, our feet sticking to the linoleum floors thick with sweat and gum and anxiety, our bums aching from hard chairs, our eyes stinging from smoke, our hands sweaty from clutching each other, our hearts fluttering a little, our limbs aching to touch, attuned to the voice booming over the loudspeaker, "Fields, move back; Friedman come to the desk."

I spent six New Years' Days in prison visiting G, and this was year seven, and I believed this would be the last.

Instead I woke up that morning—cold, bitter cold—and I knew something was wrong.

Let me set the scene. This was Ontario. By that time G was living in a prison several miles from the bungalow I bought one month before we married. I bought it because I wanted us to have a place that was ours, a place that would be a haven for G to come home to one day, a place that would comfort me and the girls.

The bungalow was funky and fabulous—lopsided, badly insulated, with chintzy yellow siding and a rickety roof, but it sat on the lip of the St. Lawrence River and from every window I could see the water and tangled vines of ivy and sumac, towering pines, lilac trees, and wide open land. Later, new neighbors bought up the little places and transformed them into mini-mansions; they tamed wild landscape into manicured lawns. But that winter our little corner of the world was still a wilderness in its way—six kilometers from a town of five thousand, Gananoque, twenty kilometers from Kingston, a limestone gem on the glittering shores of Lake Ontario.

I heated the bungalow with a woodstove so that, always in winter, and on that New Year's Day, the air felt like a thick blanket, fragrant with oak and pine. That morning I lay on the same couch I lay on every night—the couch that wasn't beautiful but was the most comfortable couch I've ever known. I stared out at the river through the sliding glass doors. On this same spot, every night for all those years, I'd sat and talked on the phone with G. Of course, I couldn't phone him—prisoners have to call out, collect. And naturally my phone bills were endless pages of collect local calls—and my left ear grew a callous, and my car always needed repair from long drives to prison. But I could never get enough of G, not even of his voice, not even when it was drenched with anger or suppressed fear, which it often was. Everything about him turned my heart inside out. Even now, even ten years since the last time I saw him, I can hear the thick sadness deep in his throat, can feel something that is no longer love but remains a kind of sweet sadness for all that was lost. But back then, back on that New Year's Day, I sat on that couch and closed my eyes and tried to imagine what it would feel like when G finally came home.

By then I may have already lost sight of who exactly I loved, but I did know we were bound together in this fight of ours to bring him home to his loved ones, to surround him in sanity, to sit with him, holding his hand, staring out at this river. To lie in bed with him so that he could listen to the cry in the distance of the loons and to the splash of the carp in the springtime river; to watch the moon rise over the river, and the sun set. To swim together, and hike together, and wake together. To watch him cooking up his famous fish stew in our kitchen and serve it on real plates. To do everything other couples did. Ordinary things. To live our lives free of guards listening in on every conversation we shared, free of strip searches, free of beginning each visit knowing that G was stripping off his hideous uniform and bending over before a hostile guard, lifting his heels, enduring all that humiliation so that he could walk into a room to hug us.

That morning I again listened to Bruce Cockburn, and I joined him in song, "You gotta kick at the darkness till it bleeds daylight."

That morning I felt terror. I was frozen in fear. And aching, as if someone had socked me in the gut. I had no breath. G hadn't phoned me the night before. New Year's Eve and no phone call, the first night in nearly seven years he hadn't phoned with the exception of those nights when the prison was locked down—when violence raged inside, sometimes for weeks at a time. During those times there was no communication. There was silence. There was fearful waiting.

So I telephoned the prison and I asked the guard who answered, "Anything wrong in there?"

"What?" he asked. I heard the bitterness in his voice, but who wouldn't feel bitter working in prison on a crisp New Year's Day?

Sometimes I did feel sorry for those guards who sat in the same dismal rooms we sat in but held nobody's hand. I felt sorry for them, and I hated them because I knew what they thought of us. They wondered about us women who loved convicts. They thought, and sometimes told us, that we were sluts, miserable garbage. They asked us how we could dare to bring children into these miserable places—and who were these kids? The older guards—men and women who had worked inside for years—understood that people are people, that some cons are cool, some not so cool, some wives are messed up human beings and some are lovely, and that some of these children—like all children—would go to Harvard, while some would rob banks, some would marry several times, some would become nuns or priests, astronauts or farmers, models or medicine men. But most of the guards despised us wives and our children, and in return we despised them.

Sometimes in my dreams I heard the echoes of their voices calling over loudspeakers, "Friedman, feet on the floor, hands to yourself," the way they did in order to humiliate us in the visiting room. But that morning on the phone, I heard in the guard's voice only his own loneliness when he said, "Nothing going on in here, lady."

I woke that morning with my heart pounding and this deep ache in my gut. G and I were always saying goodbye, and every time I said goodbye I thought, "What if something happens to him tonight?" Prisons are violent places, like the rest of the world but more so, and with no escape. "What if something happens to him?"

It was one of my mantras.

And that New Year's Day morning I knew something must have happened. Nothing would stop him from phoning me on New Year's Eve. So I said, "Excuse me, what did you say?"

He said it again. "Nothing going on in here, I said."

"Nothing? You sure? No lockdown?"

"Everything's quiet," he snapped.

"Well, is my husband in solitary then?" I held my breath. Something always happened on the cusp of big moments, and this was the year. This was parole year—six weeks shy of G's hearing and the possibility that he might be released to spend his daylight hours at home, only the nights locked up still.

I looked outside at the frozen landscape, at the ice frosting bare tree branches, at the sweep of deep, white snow, and I remembered: The day before we were to wed, the prison in which he lived—the one that was only a few miles from the bungalow I purchased so that we would be near each other—had sent him thirty kilometers away, to a higher security prison, "for the good order of the institution," and I remembered spending the next eighteen months and thousands of dollars fighting to bring him back where he belonged, fighting a bogus story administrators invented only to deter our marrying.

So on that New Year's morning I listened as the guard shuffled papers. I held my breath, waiting to hear what they had done to him. But the guard grumbled, "Nope, he's fine. In his cell. Or maybe the gym."

I felt that kick to the gut again and then, before I could stop myself, the words poured out, "But he didn't call last night." By then I knew enough never to say such things to guards, never to offer them ammunition to use against us. But I was weak-kneed, lost. Naturally the guard picked up on that.

"Nothin' I can do about that," he sneered. I could hear the sneer and smirk in his voice.

"You're sure nothing's wrong?" I asked again, and then I pinched my arm, hard. What's the matter with you, Amy? I thought.

"Nothin' wrong," he said, and then, thankfully, he hung up on me.

I sat very still. The girls were away, and I was glad for that. I needed silence. I needed solitude. I needed to find a way to breathe again. The day was cold enough to offer me an excuse not to venture outside. I rekindled the fire in the stove and inhaled the scent. I wrapped a blanket tightly around me. I called no one. I just lay there and waited for G to phone. I waited through the entire day, watching the bright blue sky turn frosty and pale, then grey, then black. I watched each star emerge, listened to the sound of snow hardening.

When the clock switched from 10 to 10:01, and I knew the prison lights were out and he wouldn't call, I tried to cry, but I must have been holding my breath; tears wouldn't come. Was G angry at me about something? Had I said or done something wrong? I replayed every visit and conversation we'd had all through those holiday weeks. I thought about the Christmases when his mom was still alive and I had somewhere to go, a family to embrace me, gifts to unwrap and gifts to give; I thought about his mother's funeral, about that day when, for the first time in a decade, G was released from prison so that he could attend his mother's funeral, wearing shackles and handcuffs, escorted by guards. I thought about how much I needed him to come home, how I couldn't spend another year in visiting rooms, couldn't spend another year supporting everyone, couldn't spend another year dreaming of real life....

Why hadn't he called?

Two days passed like that. I don't remember moving once, though I'm certain I must have showered. I may even have eaten something. Perhaps my beloved Kate stopped by. She usually did—still feisty and formidable in her eighty-third year, still driving her crazy creaky Honda, her little brown dog and her big Afghan hound in the back, still working, still bossy, still glamorous as she had been in the 1930s when she was a Hollywood movie star. She must have stopped by because Kate worried about me when she didn't hear from me. Maybe she did appear. Maybe she said something wise. She usually did. Maybe she was the first person to explain to me about how frightened prisoners can become when they face release. I do know Graham told me that—lanky and lovable Graham, director of the prisoners' rights organization, always sane and always warm, and such a friend. He's the one who told me the stories of men on the eve of parole—men he'd known who committed suicide or tried to escape or committed crimes. He explained that suddenly they would fear this freedom they'd so long craved, about how fear made them crazy and stupid.

On January third, the phone rang, and when I picked it up and heard the operator say, "Collect call fr…" I screamed. I know I screamed. "Yes, yes, yes, I accept…" and I remember the way G's voice cracked, the way he sounded even farther away than usual, so far away, out of my grasp altogether.

I said, "G, G, why…"

He stopped me. He explained that all night long on New Year's Eve he'd lain in his cell thinking about us, thinking of what was ahead, thinking he couldn't do this to me, couldn't saddle me with a husband who faced years of parole, who couldn't earn much money, who was a nobody, only a burden…

He kept talking, but I interrupted. "G, I love you. We can do this…I've spent seven years fighting for you…we can do this…don't leave me…please…give this a chance…"

I did talk him into letting me visit him that day. We stood in the hideous room hugging each other, holding each other. He held me with more longing than I'd ever been held. We kissed. We looked into each other's eyes. We smiled and wept. I gripped his hand and stared at him.

"Don't do this to us, don't leave me," I said.

He didn't. Not that day.

Not that month.

He didn't leave me for another eighteen months, not until after he'd been paroled and after he'd dived into a deep pool of depression and anger.

But even when I think of all those days and nights of sadness that followed the New Year's Eve when he first did not telephone me, I see only that sheet of snow outside the bungalow, and I feel the cold that pierced me because that was the morning I knew we were finished.

I just pretended that I didn't know.

The footprint of that wound remains, and sometimes when I look out at a field of snow or at bare branches coated in ice, I feel the stab all over again. And still, and this is what I don't understand but what I do know, somehow I feel only gratitude that I can feel that deeply, that I can hold in my heart still both the love I felt and the pain.

⁂

AMY FRIEDMAN HAS PUBLISHED two memoirs, *Kick the Dog and Shoot the Cat* and *Nothing Sacred*. But since she published them in Canada, where she was a well-known newspaper columnist, prison activist, and shepherd, the books aren't easy to find. Easier to find is her syndicated newspaper column of children's stories, "Tell Me A Story," which can be read in newspapers throughout the world and CDs featuring the stories. Amy teaches "Writing the Personal Essay," "Creative Nonfiction," and a new course, "From Page to Stage," at UCLA Extension. Amy is currently writing a memoir entitled *Sweet Talker* about the prison years.

Mary Ann Reynolds

Margaret

WHAT IS THIS RESISTANCE I have to going there again, procrastinating writing about my personal grief? What comes to mind is a scene from Beth Henley's play *Crimes of the Heart*, made into a movie with Diane Keeton, Jessica Lange, and Sissy Spacek, in which Old Granddaddy has been dying for a long time, and the three Southern sisters have just been through so much—parental abandonment, suicide, sacrifice, numbing out, lies, neglect, loneliness, scandal, attempted murder, and gallons of too-sweet lemonade—that by the time they learn that Old Granddaddy has finally died, they burst out laughing.

An evening out with girlfriends, taking turns reading favorite Rumi poems on the patio of a Mexican restaurant, and laughing a lot will also do the trick.

Now I'm back home, facing it. So here it is: I am fifty-four-years old, and I can tell you that without a doubt, the most grievous thing that happened in my life was the murder of my younger sister Margaret when I was eleven years old.

This is a story about trauma, about experiencing a loss that is so horrifying that I thought, "If this is what life is, I don't want to be here." I checked out in some ways. Yet here I am, years later, and, damn, that was a high price to pay. Never again.

So here's the story. One day, right before she was to start first grade, Margaret went outside to play after lunch. She went down the street to visit a neighbor girl, but the girl was taking a nap and her mother told Margaret to come back later.

Margaret walked down the alley back towards our house. She met a fifteen-year-old neighbor boy whom none of my family knew. He was also walking down the alley and they began walking together. That was the last anyone except that boy saw of Margaret alive.

I don't know what all happened. I suspect he raped her and she was not cooperative. Maybe she threatened to tell, her most powerful weapon with her older siblings. Whatever. He strangled her with electrical wire. He strangled her for a long time, the paper said afterwards. Then he put her body in a cardboard box and covered it with leaves and trash and closed the box and left it in the woods. The paper said that the police found a trail of blood leading from his garage across the alley into the woods. There was a photo of a policeman standing by a box in the woods at night. The paper also said that the boy told the police that she was still breathing when he put her into the box.

Margaret and I shared a room from the time she got out of the crib until that day. She had straight brown hair and big blue eyes and sucked her two middle fingers. She still wet the bed sometimes. She was also daring. She once looked up a nun's habit to see her artificial leg, something none of us older children would have risked. The nun just laughed and later gave her a teddy bear. And Margaret was outgoing. She was the one who told her first grade class, gathered for a group photo at orientation, to say cheese. She couldn't say her Rs, so if you asked her what her name was, you'd hear "Maw-gwet."

Every year I remember her on her birthday, May 7. I count how old she'd be now and I wonder what she'd be like if she had lived. Would we be close? Would we live in the same city? What would she have done with her life? Would she have married; would she have had children? What kind of work would she be doing?

Sometimes she shows up in my dreams, always as a young child. I miss having a sister. I had one for six years.

When my daughter turned seven, I breathed a sigh of relief. When my granddaughter turned seven, my daughter and I both breathed sighs of relief. *She made it past six. Whew.*

I also remember Margaret every year on her death day, September 4. That date is seared into my memory. I feel sad, and it passes. After forty-three years, my grief has been reduced to feeling what a horrible shame it was that she died like that. She just happened to run into that boy on that day, and he just happened to be so unstable that he had a psychotic break and he killed her. I so wish that she had been able to die at peace, in the presence of love. I wish that for you, for me, and for everyone.

But there's more to my grief than that.

Now I grieve more for myself as an eleven-year-old, encountering a loss so big I could never, no matter how hard I tried, have imagined it. It was as if the rug of my life, of everything that gave me security and confidence, was pulled out from under my feet, and I fell into a dark scary void.

My father had told us that she was dead and the police suspected a neighbor boy. Then we kids were farmed out to friends of the family so my parents could grieve and make funeral arrangements. No one was telling me what was going on with Margaret or my parents. In a house full of children, someone left a newspaper out. Alone in a hallway, I spied it and saw the front page headline, "Child's Body Found in Box Near Creek." I read the article. *This is about my sister.* I learned about the trail of blood, the strangulation, the boy's confession. I saw my name listed with my family's names, as survivors. I went deeper into shock. I wanted to go home, but home would never be the same. Sometimes it seems like my life since then has been about finding home.

We children were not taken to see her body. I remember my family being shown to the front pew in the church for her funeral. The church was packed. I kept turning around to look at a small white wicker coffin at the back of the church. *My sister's in that box. I need to get her out.* Pause. *But all these people are behaving like it's her funeral. I don't know what to believe.* And perceiving at eleven the irony of a church full of people singing Margaret's favorite hymn, "All Things Bright and Beautiful." *No, they're not.*

Then the burial. It was the most awful feeling in the world to leave the cemetery, leaving Margaret behind. *I am helpless.*

The next day I started sixth grade at a new school where I didn't know anyone in my class. They all, of course, knew that my sister had died. They all looked at me when the principal showed me to my classroom after school had already started. No one said anything. I just wanted to melt into the floor. *I don't want to be known for this. Not for this.*

My mother told me a few weeks after Margaret's death that a judge had committed the boy who killed her to the state hospital. I thought there would be a trial, like on television. I never laid eyes on him or even knew his name. Just that he was big for his age, according to the paper. *I am small. I am a girl.*

My family stopped talking about Margaret because we were just too fragile. We just hunkered down into our prescribed roles and got through, with a huge hole where Margaret used to be.

Of course I had post-traumatic stress disorder. Anyone could figure that out, and when something like that happens nowadays, counselors would appear out of the woodwork offering support. But back then, in the 1960s, no one knew.

I became hyper-vigilant. I couldn't trust life. I could run faster than any of the girls in the sixth grade because I had a very good reason to be fast, to be able to get away from murderers.

Fast forward through time. I went into therapy in the 1980s. I got a young, inexperienced therapist who diagnosed me with depression. I told him at the start that I had unresolved grief over my sister's death. He just didn't get it, that I needed to talk about it; he wanted to avoid it. I finally left, re-traumatized and humiliated, thinking if this is what therapy is, I don't want it.

At forty-eight, after both of my parents had died, I started having vivid dreams and a constant feeling of anxiety. I went into therapy again, choosing a therapist with much care. This therapist diagnosed me with post-traumatic stress disorder. That was a beautiful gift, in hindsight.

Then I was laid off from my high tech job with severance pay and ended therapy. For two months, I processed by myself, dreaming, inviting memories back, feeling, naming, putting fragments of memories into order, and writing intensely, digging deeply to get the full story. There were times when I didn't bathe or change clothes for several days, fluctuating between despair and curiosity. I slept poorly and at odd hours, but something within was pushing me to heal and grow.

I reworked memories, imagining crawling quietly from our front pew around the side to Margaret's coffin in the back of the church, opening it, and finding her peacefully dead, there but not there, and accepting her death. I imagined riding in on a white horse and rescuing her from the murderer before she had been harmed, blowing the murderer's brains out, and coolly blowing the smoke off my gun as I rode away with her. Yes, I am a murderer, too, in my imagination, but at least in my imagination, I am not helpless.

I talked to my brothers about their memories. I looked up the priest, Father Hartwell, who had conducted Margaret's funeral and had been with us when my father told us that Margaret was dead, murdered. He was helpful. Turned out he had had a second career as a psychologist in a VA hospital and was very familiar with PTSD. He remembered things I didn't.

I also called up a woman who had lived next door to my family when Margaret died. I hadn't seen Mrs. Flowers since I was a teenager. I met with her and another former neighbor, Mrs. King. They were very helpful, filling in more of the missing pieces, including the name of the murderer.

I looked him up in the phone book and he was listed. Lives a few miles from me.

Through a nonprofit that helps crime victims, I learned that he had spent time in prison in the 1970s. So he was punished after all. He served his time and never went back. That's all I needed to know. I felt safer in this world. He is not the same person now as he was at fifteen, just like I am not the same person I was at eleven. I wish him peace.

I read a book, *Waking the Tiger*, about PTSD actually being a physical energy block like what an animal experiences when it's been attacked by a predator, a numbing to prepare it for death. If the animal survives, it rejoins the herd and shakes and trembles to regain its equilibrium, and then it just moves on with its life. People don't know how to do that and usually need help. One day, my body spontaneously released the energy block from the trauma. I shook and trembled in my bed for a few minutes, and that was a very big deal toward regaining my wholeness.

On September fourth of that year, I held a celebration of my sister's life, attended by family, friends, and the priest. It meant a lot to me to be able to do that, no matter how many years it had been since Margaret died.

There is an uneasiness associated with experiencing a trauma like this, of not knowing if you have ever really gotten to the bottom of it. I've done the best I can, but when I get blindsided by someone I trust, it can trigger me, and I really don't like that. I did a Neuro-Linguistic Programming trauma procedure earlier this year that helped me put the trauma more firmly in the past. Since then, I've experienced a freedom from anxiety and a confidence that I can get on with my life that is remarkable.

That's where I am with it now. I've learned some important lessons: Horrible things can happen in life, and healing is possible. The only way around is through. If I need help, I find it.

MARY ANN REYNOLDS, FIFTY-FIVE, lives near downtown Austin, Texas, in a one hundred and two-year-old house with her nineteen-year-old cat. Her varied education—degrees from the University of Oklahoma and UT Austin and certifications in technical writing, InterPlay leadership, and master practitioner of NLP—contributes to her work as a publisher, editor, and coach. Besides practicing yoga, meditation, and ecstatic dance, Mary Ann takes delight in walking to work and longer journeys. She counts personal transformation, including shamanic practices and enlightenment, among her deepest fascinations, and she treasures her beautiful daughter Lela, lively granddaughter Hannah, and the company of dear friends.

Hope Edelman

Kaddish *in Topanga*

THE BOULDER WAS MONSTROUSLY large, freakishly large, like some kind of extraterrestrial castoff that had crash-landed right in the middle of Topanga Canyon Boulevard. Under any other circumstances, I might have viewed this as a uniquely Southern Californian twist on the Sisyphean myth—how man's attempt to master nature always results in nature crashing back down and completely blocking traffic in the process—but this particular January the boulder just felt like bad luck on top of bad luck.

Los Angeles was having the rainiest stretch it had seen in one hundred years. I'd missed most of it by spending the past three weeks in New York, helping my father die. My brother, sister, and I had been at his bedside every day, supervising his health aide, consulting with the hospice nurses, coordinating the burial plans. Then the day after the funeral, I opened the *New York Times* at my brother's kitchen table to find a photo of a twenty-five-foot boulder blocking my route home.

Hardscrabble, resourceful living has always been part of the Topanga Canyon way, but this was ridiculous. Just getting back from the airport was going to require a circuitous nighttime route through the back roads of Malibu that I didn't think I had the stamina for. Not to mention getting to or from anywhere else once I finally made it home.

"*Shit*," I said, loudly, in front of the girls.

My seven-year-old daughter Maya raised her eyebrows slightly, and then went back to her bowl of Cheerios. Her younger sister Eden didn't even look up. We'd been through too much in the past three weeks—adult diapers and morphine syringes and my father laid out in a plain wooden casket with little fabric Xs resting on his eyes—to care about an errant expletive here or there.

Here's what I knew that Monday morning in New York: My father, my last parent, was dead. Los Angeles was one big mudslide waiting to happen. And a two-ton boulder was sitting between me and my home.

Here's what I didn't yet know: This boulder was also sitting in the way of ten Jews and me.

If you were raised in the New York suburbs in the 1970s by an orthodox Jewish mother; grew up using separate dishes for dairy and meat, had a *Bat Mitzvah* at age thirteen (a much smaller and far more modest party than all your friends had, a fact you still feel compelled to mention nearly thirty years after the fact), buried your mother in a Jewish cemetery when you were seventeen, and grew up to marry an Israeli and send your kids to Hebrew school once a week even though your religious beliefs now tilt more toward Buddhism than Judaism, what you do when your father dies is say *Kaddish*. The impulse is as automatic, even as unconscious, as that.

Kaddish is the mourner's prayer, recited throughout *shiva*, the seven-day period of Jewish mourning that follows a funeral. It begins like a mournful wail, then morphs into a determined chant: first the outpouring of grief, then the vehement decision to keep soldiering on. *Yitgadal v'yitgadash, sh'may rabah.* Reciting it at my brother's house the night of our father's funeral dredged up images from some unconscious vault of my childhood—of my grandmother in a brown wool beret, fingering her prayer book with arthritic knuckles in the women's section of her *shul*; of Mrs. Hazelkorn shouting, "*Sheket, B'vakashah!*" at the Aleph class to get us to calm down. After so many years of yoga and meditation, I was amazed that all of that was still *in* there.

We read the prayer out loud from Xeroxed pamphlets the funeral director had the foresight to see we would need. My siblings and I had opted for the small, dark, Orthodox Jewish mortuary in the middle of our hometown instead of the modern, nondenominational funeral home out by the highway with its Italian funeral director and mauve and gray designer décor. Our father had a complicated relationship with Judaism when he was alive and hadn't been anything close to observant, more like went along with it to keep peace when my mother was alive and abandoned it all after she died. Nevertheless. When the time came to bury him, my brother, sister, and I surprised ourselves by going for every bit of it: the simple, wooden coffin, the ritual purification and preparation of the corpse, the white burial robe, even a paid *shomer* to sit and say prayers over the body all night.

"I don't want him to be alone," my sister said. I knew what she meant. He'd already been a widower for twenty-four years when he died.

I don't know what my father would have said about such a profoundly Jewish send-off. He wasn't a man of strong opinions. He preferred to avoid conflict of any form. And we were three strong-willed children, a function of necessity rather than choice. After our mother died, our father provided for us, made sure we had clothing, food, and a place to live, but from the moment we returned from the hospital without her in 1981, he assumed the posture of a collapsed man. I knew, even then, he had begun to hand our raising over to us.

I filled out my college applications that fall, signed his name on the checks, and the following September flew off to Chicago alone. Two years later, my friend backed out of a scheduled cross-country road trip, leaving me to drive to an internship in Oregon myself. I called my father, hoping he'd offer to pay for an airline ticket. Instead, he told me to drive safe and have fun. Every night when I called from a different motel along I-80, he wanted to know what I'd seen that day. "Write it all down," he said. I still can't believe he let me make the drive alone.

But that was the unspoken arrangement between us: I did what I wanted, and he didn't get in my way. Or maybe he was just too sad and depressed to intervene. Soon after my mother died, he began a steady retreat into solitude, kept company only by a handful of co-workers, two tumblers of Dewar's in the evenings, and the *New York Times* crossword puzzle on Sunday afternoons. Years later, after he sobered up and retired, he spent his time roaming the aisles of Wal-Mart looking for bargains and watching DVDs on the home theater system he installed in his two-bedroom apartment. He encouraged his adult children to travel and take risks, but rarely left his own town. His needs were simple: heat in the winter, air conditioning in the summer, a new Chevy Bronco leased every three years. When he called me once a week he asked about the weather, or my car, and what funny things my daughters had said since we last spoke. But because he wasn't the strong, decisive father I wanted him to be, I barely made room for him to be a father at all. I almost never called him, except in those final months. I didn't like bad news either, but I had to get past that. By the summer of 2004, there was plenty of bad news to smear around. It was a particularly deadly liver tumor. A year at the most, the doctors said. He made it seven months.

⁂

To get home from LAX, we had to overshoot Topanga Canyon Boulevard by four miles and then backtrack through the Malibu hills in the rain. Roads winding up the mountain like serpentine ribbons were slick with mud and littered with rocks. In a few places the shoulder had started to crumble over the drop off. The route would have been treacherous enough in daylight. It was damn near suicidal in the dark. When the four of us finally walked through our front door safely, my shoulders dropped two inches.

By then, it was Wednesday night. We'd spent the first two nights of *shiva* at my brother's house, reciting *Kaddish* with the required *minyan* of ten Jewish men assembled for the prayer. Two nights. It had been sufficient for me—affirming that *I am Jewish, yes, and doing the right thing here.* Back in California, the rote practicalities of homeownership and family life took over. I made phone calls to see if the school bus was running, mopped up a leak that had sprung in the family room wall, and called a contractor for an estimate. My husband braved the roads back down to LAX to fly to a high-tech conference in San Jose.

A Topanga friend on our side of the boulder came for dinner Thursday night, and we spent the evening drinking wine and talking about my father: about his passion for crossword puzzles, his bravery in hospice care, and the way he could do the best Donald Duck impressions you'd ever heard. He would entertain all my friends by talking with what sounded like a mouth full of bubbles. Remembering him as that kind of father, the one I'd known before tragedy felled him, hurt in a way I hadn't anticipated.

The rain tapered off for half a day, then started again in earnest. I kept the kids home from school on Friday and fumbled around the house, folding laundry and paying bills that had piled up in my absence, manufacturing small moments of purpose to fill time so I couldn't obsess about the hollow, carved-out feeling that had established residence beneath my ribs. By Jewish law I was in mourning for another two days, and as I walked from room to room, I was pursued by the nagging idea I should be doing something to acknowledge this. But the absence of family and friends around me made any solitary attempts at mourning feel pathetic, lonely, even pointless, somehow.

Still, I wanted to do something. *Something.* The girls and I set up a little altar for my father in the living room, placing his 1952 Army portrait alongside a photograph of him at my brother's wedding in 1999. In front of the photos, I lit the memorial candle my friend had brought for me, and we said our goodbyes out loud. It didn't feel like a profound gesture, or enough, but it was a start.

And then it was Friday evening, the sixth night of *shiva*, and I was homebound with the kids for the weekend. Over dinner, we discussed how we might spend our time. Maya wanted movie nights with popcorn. Eden wanted a play date with kids down the road. "What do you want, Mom?" Maya asked, and I thought about it for a moment. And then I knew. I wanted to say *Kaddish* for my father, in my own house, before time ran out.

Normally, finding a *minyan* of ten Jewish men to show up for dinner on the west side of L.A. on twenty-four-hours' notice isn't a daunting task. It's quite a bit harder with a boulder in the middle of a main access road. It was clear I would have to draw the *minyan* within Topanga, plus the few friends who would be willing to drive the back roads in the rain.

Topanga Canyon: "Alternative" doesn't begin to describe the place. It's a small, unincorporated town in the Santa Monica Mountains filled with filmmakers, artists, musicians, and a sprinkling of aging bohemians who like to evoke the halcyon days when Neil Young and Little Feat lived among us. Solstice celebrations and Earth Day are among our biggest events of the year. Three hundred people showed up at a town hall meeting to protest the town's first traffic light. Let's just say, it's not the kind of place where organized religion rules.

Years ago, I saw an episode of *Northern Exposure* in which residents of Cicely, Alaska, tried to round up ten Jews so Dr. Fleischman could say *Kaddish* for his uncle. An unlikely assortment of Alaskans arrived at his door one by one, by snowshoe and bush plane, sporting month-old beards and clutching their *Bar Mitzvah* ware. I sensed I might be in for an episode like that.

I started with an email blitz to every Topangan in my online address book. It felt like writing a bizarre personal ad. Wanted: *Ten Jews for one hour Saturday night. Dinner provided. Non-observant okay.* Rachel, a local writer friend, picked right up on the request. For the first time in years she was dating a Jewish man, she said, and could finally put this to good use. They'd both come, and she'd forward my email to all the other writers we knew.

"Aimee Bender is Jewish," she said. "I'll try her. And Janet Fitch. She's all the way over in Silver Lake, but you never know."

"Janet Fitch is Jewish?" How did Rachel know this? I couldn't help feeling impressed.

Within an hour I was receiving emails from authors I barely knew, expressing condolences and regrets that they couldn't make the drive safely in the rain. I got on the phone, calling everyone I could think of with a Jewish background, observant or not. Mehran up the street said he had earlier plans he couldn't get out of, but he'd try to be there by eight. Stacey called back to say she and her husband (non-Jewish) would pick up food on the way. That made five, including me. Jeff, an old friend from high school who hadn't set foot in a synagogue in years, said he'd drive the hour-and-a-half loop from Santa Monica all the way around through the Valley. Six Jews. Sue would drive up the hill from her house; her husband, who was Catholic, wanted to come, too. Seven Jews. The speed with which people agreed when they heard the word *Kaddish* was swift. Some kind of deep, ancient nerve had been struck, among Jews and non-Jews alike, asked to be counted on to pray for the dead.

Then I remembered Steve, my neighbor with the vineyard that borders our land, who I was pretty sure once mentioned he was half-Jewish. Turned out it was a quarter, through his father's mother, his German wife explained when I called. She promised to send him over if he fit my criteria, though she was sure he'd never done this kind of thing before.

My criteria? What *was* my criteria? From the start, I'd decided to disband with the Orthodox gender restriction; it seemed ridiculous to exclude myself from the tally of ten. But once I'd loosened this rule, what kept me from loosening others? I'd never had more than a passing interest in my friends' religious affiliations before, beyond who followed what tradition, so I didn't send the wrong kind of holiday card, but now their degree of—how to say this?—*Jewishness* had become of intense interest to me. Was Steve, who was one-fourth Jewish, Jewish *enough*? And what about Stacey's husband, who had gone all the way through conversion classes but stopped short of actually converting, even though he belonged to a synagogue and observed the Jewish holidays with more enthusiasm and commitment than I? An uncomfortable sense of elitism emerged from pointing an affirming finger at one friend but not another, and it was impossible to go through this kind of exercise without the ick factor of recalling a darker, historical selection process that took place not all that long ago.

Oh, the hell with it, I decided. It was my *minyan*, after all. Steve counted. Stacey's husband counted. Anyone who wanted to come counted, Jewish or not. Dr. Fleischman came to the same conclusion when he decided to invite all the residents of Cicely to recite *Kaddish* for his uncle. A community of mourners should be bound by intention, not by religion of birth. Amen.

In the end, fourteen adults and four children assembled in my living room that Saturday night. They were the intrepid, the determined, the loyal, and the ones with 4x4 SUVs: six-foot-tall Rachel and her six-foot-four boyfriend, dressed for cocktails; Steve in his mud-spattered Wellingtons; Gonen and Yael hurrying to the front door to beat the rain clutching handfuls of *yarmulkes* from their son's recent *Bar Mitzvah*. No one could remember how a *minyan* was supposed to stand, so we arranged ourselves in a large circle between the couch and the dining room table. It reminded me of the closing circle at the Adult Children of Alcoholics meetings I attended in my twenties, the place where I finally began to accept my father for who he was, and tried to start forgiving him for not being who I needed him to be. We said the Lord's Prayer at the end of each ACOA meeting, a recitation that eventually became as much a part of my inner landscape as the Hebrew prayer over wine, and ended with the Serenity Prayer, which turned out to be a pretty good prayer at a time of grief as well: *God, grant me the serenity to accept the things I cannot change; the courage to change the things I can; and the wisdom to know the difference.*

It took my father a lot of courage to sober up in his sixties. When he showed up at his inaugural AA meeting, I admired him for the first time. At the very end, when I sat by his bedside and told him I would miss him and meant it, we were just who we were to each other, nothing more: the daughter who had the moxie to drive across the country by herself at twenty, and the father who trusted her enough to let her go. Only much later, as a parent myself, did I understand how appealing the idea of getting in a car and driving through prairies and mountain ranges all the way to the sea, with the windows rolled down and the hot wind rushing through your hair, must have been to a widower with three children, a mortgage, and a repetitive day job. Only then did I realize how happy it must have made him for those four days to imagine me out there with all that unbridled freedom, on the open road.

Gonen recited *Kaddish* in his native Hebrew, while everyone listened in rapt respect. Stacey read the English translation with tears streaming down her cheeks—Stacey, my friend since the eighth grade, who knew my father back when he was still my father, before he became a facsimile of who he once used to be.

I looked around the circle at these people who'd driven through rain and mud and around an impenetrable boulder to be in my living room that night. I'd like to say my father would have been proud of my efforts to bring them together, but that may still be the daughter in me trying to impress the father I never had. In truth, I think my father would have found the whole thing hilarious. He would have seen it as a great story.

"Write it all down," he would have said.

Hope Edelman

❧ ❧ ❧

HOPE EDELMAN IS THE author of four nonfiction books, including the best-sellers *Motherless Daughters* and *Motherless Mothers.* Her work has appeared in numerous magazines, newspapers, and anthologies, including *The Bitch in The House*, *Toddler*, and *Blindsided by a Diaper.* She lives in Topanga Canyon, California, with her husband and two daughters.

Katherine Tanney

The End of Grief

THE LAST CONVERSATION I had with my mother before she died was on New Year's Eve. I was in my living room in Austin, Texas, and she was a patient at UCLA Medical Center, a surprisingly drab hospital located in one of Los Angeles's most affluent areas. Before I picked up the phone, I opened my bottle of sparkling wine, purchased earlier that day on ceremony. It was four-thirty in the afternoon and I couldn't wait to start sipping farewell to the year that had marked the death of my father from Alzheimer's and Bush's mind boggling reelection.

I expected a nurse to answer the phone, to say that Mrs. Tanney couldn't talk but that she, the nurse, would let her know I had called. I was looking for something quick and guilt-relieving when I pressed the hospital's number, but it turned out my uncle's email was wrong. She'd been moved from the Intensive Care Unit to her own room, which meant we'd probably be able to speak.

"I'll transfer you," the nurse said.

In another moment my mother picked up, her voice ragged and terribly weak.

"Hi, Mom; it's Kath."

I'd been to visit her in early December, the first time we'd seen each other in three years. My sister Dina was with me and the two of us walked right past the frail, white haired old woman struggling to breathe through an oxygen mask without recognizing our own mother. After twenty minutes of staring at her unconscious face and adjusting to the shock of what she had become, we removed our gloves and gowns, left the ICU, and went out to lunch.

It was gorgeous outside. The sky was blue, the temperature in the low seventies. As we walked through Westwood Village, we recalled countless Saturday afternoons as kids, going in and out of shops no longer there. Now in our forties—Dina, a doctor with a husband and toddler waiting for her in northern California, and me, a struggling writer between jobs, between romances—we agreed on California Pizza Kitchen, which had replaced a decades-old local Italian restaurant. At a table outside, we tossed around ideas for a book, eating and brainstorming, and getting rather giddy.

"It's strange that we're having so much fun while our mother's a few blocks away, close to death," Dina said.

If there was one thing I'd finally learned, it was to accept my feelings without judgment. I knew what it looked like to lose someone you adored, to fear and pre-mourn that loss. I'd seen friends go through it and had experienced it myself when my maternal grandmother passed away. That pain showed me I was all right, that I could feel the full range of human emotions. So I said, "We've already experienced our grief. We've spent our whole lives wishing for the kind of mother we never had. We're stuffing our faces and dreaming of a book project because we lost our mother a long time ago."

So much for tidy wisdom. I began crying uncontrollably as soon as we got back and were faced once more with her ravaged state, with legs that looked like a skeleton's beneath the blanket. Though her eyes were open a slit, it was impossible to tell if she was remotely cognizant.

"I'm sorry," I blubbered, almost laughing with embarrassment. I was speaking to my mother, excusing myself for being so emotional when she was the one hooked up to half a dozen wires and tubes. I was also speaking to Dina, apologizing for my inconsistency. I didn't know *why* I was crying. Even in my tears, I didn't have any love left for my mother. Perhaps it was over what happens to all of us, to our once strong bodies. My mother, as I'd known and feared and loathed her, had been demolished.

"Do you remember that I came to visit you a few weeks ago?" I asked on the phone New Year's Eve.

"Yes. You looked like a Quaker minister."

Drinking my champagne and looking out the window at the front lawns and trees of my neighborhood, I imagined Quaker ministers were austere, intense and bony, like Abraham Lincoln. I am lean and stand over six feet tall. When my mother saw me at the hospital, I was sporting what was for her a new and very short haircut that barely grazed the collar of my Navy pea coat.

"You say the nicest things," I said.

It was easy to be generous now, to forgive and overlook and pretend. It was unlikely my mother would leave the hospital alive, if only because she'd been there too long. Dina said the odds were not good. There were too many mistakes waiting to happen and opportunistic infections known to grow in the very tubes she was hooked up to. No one was looking after her but the hospital staff. She'd been alone for months, without family or friends—her friends had fallen away over the years—to encourage and monitor her recovery.

I put my feet up and started to relax. "Tonight's New Year's Eve," I said. "Did you know that?"

"It is?"

I wondered what other news I could tell her to fill the time. I started with the Indian Ocean quake and tsunami, which, it turned out, she'd heard about on the television above her bed.

"Are you married?" she suddenly asked. She'd asked me the same question after regaining consciousness in the ICU. Dina had gone home by then, missing the chance to speak to our mother, but I'd stayed several days more, to see old friends, go to the flea market, visit the ocean. Now, on the phone, I repeated that it was just me and the dogs in my cozy little home and that I was happy.

"But I still like men," I reassured her. I was thinking of the Quaker minister remark. "In case you're worried that I'm a lesbian."

The only other time I'd cut off my long thick hair was back in art school; it had been such a distressing event for my mother that she urged me to get psychological counseling, the implication being that I was conflicted about my sexuality. I believe her exact words were, "Why would you do this to yourself when the women in Los Angeles try as hard as they can to look delicious?"

This time she calmly said, "I don't care if you're a lesbian."

That's when I knew something was wrong, that I was talking to a fantasy version of my mother, who was, after all, a somewhat disoriented hospital patient. Yet I couldn't help myself. A little flame ignited inside of me and I became indefensibly happy. It was New Year's Eve and my mother had been transformed into somebody loving and easy.

"Do you need any money?" she asked.

One of us had to be hallucinating. The words and the caring way she spoke them—did I need any money?—were straight out of her mother's mouth. My grandmother had died six years earlier but at that moment she was right there, speaking through my mother.

"No," I said, "but I love that you asked." She'd never been one to worry about the needs of others, especially when it came to money.

"Is there *anything* you need?" she continued.

I needed a witness, a slap in the face, a helpful finger to push my jaw back into place. What is it called when you finally receive the words you've dreamed of hearing, every one of them, from the person you've given up ever hearing them from?

"I'm okay," I said.

"I used to think money was everything, but I don't care about it anymore. It's not important."

It wasn't funny any longer. I wanted the gods of heartbreaking eleventh hour conversions to cut it out. They'd discovered my secret script and shown my mother all of her lines.

"Let's you and me take a trip," she said.

"Where?" By then I was fully immersed in the sparkling pool of sudden good intentions between us.

"I'd like to drive across the Italian countryside in a sports car."

Thank God for the imagination. There was my pathetic mother, helpless in a hospital bed. Twice she'd been cut open in the span of two months, once for heart surgery, then for a sternectomy. She was a muscle-less mass, unable even to cough up the mucus in her chest without a machine and a nurse. Her kidneys were failing due to an infection, so she was also on dialysis.

"A sports car, huh?" I saw the little car zooming on a dirt road in Tuscany, my formerly strong mother at the wheel, her brunette hair blowing wildly. When my sisters and I were in grade school, she drove a tiny MGB convertible, impractical for taking three children anywhere. Only two of us could fit in that car at a time, one squeezed without a seatbelt on the ledge in back that was intended for a sack of groceries or a handbag.

"We could go to Italy," I said, "but I'd rather see a country I haven't been to before."

She asked where I wanted to go and I was too distracted by the act of pretending I would travel *anyplace* with my mother, and by the need to reassure myself that the trip would never happen, to actually think. Finally, I mentioned Greece.

"I love you," she said out of nowhere, like someone who really means it.

Eight days later, I got a call from Dina. She'd heard from the hospital that Mom had declined all lifesaving treatment. Papers had been signed and she would likely die within the next couple of days. I was speechless. It seemed inconceivable that the woman I'd spoken with a week earlier had chosen to give up the fight. We'd been so chummy and future-oriented. I offered to help her sell her big house and get her set up when she got better. It was so damned hopeful and redemptive and important for me, even if she did think she was ninety-two.

"You're not ninety-two," I gently corrected her. "You're sixty-nine." But she didn't believe me. I got the feeling she was almost happy, or proud, of ninety-two.

Both of my sisters called her after that, for the last time. They reported that she was vile—cold and unyielding to the end. Dina said, "I love you, Mom," and received nothing back. Liz, my older sister, did the same and was asked, "How come you never showed it?"

I didn't have the guts to face *that* mother, who might leave me with lacerating words for the rest of my life. Clearly, the soft one, the maternal, nurturing woman I'd managed to connect with for an hour on New Year's Eve was gone for good, so I never said goodbye to my mother.

Five months later, with the news long digested that she'd left her entire, rather substantial estate to an art museum in Los Angeles, I was home slaving away on a freelance writing assignment. The job required that I turn high school social studies courses into light-hearted dialogue to be spoken by four well-adjusted, animated teens I'd helped create. They were: a Muslim girl, a Latino boy, a White hippie chick, and a Native American science nerd. The town they lived in, also partly my doing, was safe, friendly, and prosperous—the kind of place teens could spend their waking hours getting high on knowledge and doing good deeds and drinking health food shakes at the corner "soda" shop.

I was sitting in front of the computer screen, slogging through a poorly explained lesson on the history of communism when it occurred to me I ought to kill myself. The thought wasn't any different from an impulse to get up and make lunch or pay a visit to the bathroom. It even had a voice. "You're done," it said, watching me like a nosy neighbor at the window. "Why not go do it right now?"

I wasn't depressed at the time. I had plenty to live for, be thankful for, and yet the voice was remarkably compelling, frightening me and making me very sad to be sharing my body with it. I imagined I had something in common with schizophrenics. Then, a week later, the thought returned, but rather than let it scare me this time, I decided to examine what might be behind it.

My mother's heart attack, and the subsequent news that she wasn't expected to survive it, had initially left me ready to be struck by lightning or destroyed in a head-on collision. I told my closest friends, "Why would the universe permit me to go on living without my mother in it to torment me?" At the same time, I had almost tasted my liberation from our impossible-to-fix relationship, from the awareness of her presence on the planet and its implied rebuke of me. (She didn't want her pregnancy with me. She told me enough times in my youth, "I hate you," or "I wish I'd had an abortion," to doom her great desire, later in life, to be my friend.) So why wasn't I overjoyed to be free of her? Why, instead of skipping, as if over yellow bricks, and singing, "Ding dong, the witch is dead," was I just going through the motions of every day?

The answer came quickly: "What's my motivation?" For more than four decades, I'd succeeded at one thing after another—making friends, attracting men, excelling in art and writing, music and the workplace—in order to prove that I was lovable, that I deserved to be alive. "I'll show them" was my mantra and it extended way beyond my parents. It became the reason I did almost everything. But then my audience of two went and died on me and there I still was, toiling and striving—for what? I had no idea.

I write this on September the eleventh, six years after the attacks in New York and Washington, D.C., which will always be associated for me, to some degree, with my mother. I was asleep that long ago morning and heard her voice on the answering machine:

"Kathy, it's Mom. Pick up…pick up the phone, please; I know you're there."

I lay in bed enjoying her useless pleas, deeply grateful I hadn't answered the phone.

"The country is under attack," she said. "The World Trade Center and the Pentagon are burning!"

I thought, "Man, she'll say anything to get me to pick up." But she kept pleading and I finally got on the line. Then I turned on the TV and witnessed, in silent horror, both of the towers, one after the other, eventually collapse to rubble.

KATHERINE TANNEY IS A freelance journalist, essayist, and author of the novel, *Carousel of Progress.* Her essays have appeared in *Dirty Words: A Literary Anthology of Sex* and *Modern Love: 50 True and Extraordinary Tales of Desire, Deceit, and Devotion.*

Margaret Moser

Married to the Tattoo Mob

IN MAY OF 2006, a former lover and friend committed suicide in a particularly poignant way: He visited with his friends and family over a period of time then took his gun and drove to the graveyard where his parents were long buried. Sitting in the car outside the cemetery, he put the gun to his head and pulled the trigger.

I was devastated. We'd ceased being lovers twenty-five years before but we'd remained close friends. I often reviewed his work over the years, interviewed him on occasion, and kept the feelings warm. After his death, I was called upon to edit a section of the newspaper dedicated to him and his art. Within the many sections, I wrote about my relationship with him, trying to bear in mind that it would be read by those who knew him as well as those who didn't.

What I didn't expect was a near-hysterical call from his wife. She believed that her husband and I had carried on after they were married. It wasn't true; we'd been done and over with before they even met. In her horrific grief—and perhaps a measure of understandable guilt because their marriage was rocky—she focused on me. Alternately screaming and weeping, she sobbed about her pain and frustration and anger and bewilderment.

As best I could, I reassured her repeatedly that there had been nothing between me and her husband during their courtship, marriage, or anytime since. I tried to soothe her fears and frustrations, offering the empathy of my dad's suicide. In the end, somewhat calmer and a little mollified, we ended the conversation on a mildly positive note.

Afterward, I sat in my office at home in front of the computer and stared out the window for a long time. Across the street, little kids scampered in the driveway of my neighbor Susie, their Mexican grandmother who regularly presents me with helpings of beans and tamales. The postman drove up and filled the mailbox. I watched a dog relieve itself on the neighbor's lawn and trot off with its tail wagging. All of these benign incidents seemed to say, "Life goes on. Yes, it does."

Yes, it does.

❧ ❧ ❧

Less than a year later, on a tender green April morning in 2007, an email popped up into my computer from my friend Kandi. I returned the call.

"Rollo's dead. I don't know any other way to say it. I'm sorry."

Her words cut to the bone. He'd killed himself with a gun, just like his mother did. Just like my father did.

The pain was exquisite.

❧ ❧ ❧

Rollo Banks and I were married December 4, 1984, less than three months after our first date. We stayed married for fifteen years and with the exception of a couple periods of estrangement in the early 90s and around the divorce in 1999, we remained very close. For the last few years, I'd been editing his "Tattoo Tales," a series of stories from his thirty-plus years in the business being printed in a popular tattoo magazine. I knew these stories backward and forward, so it was a pleasure to edit them.

Born as Michael Malone in San Rafael, California, in 1942, Rollo was a modern master of classic American and Oriental style tattooing. He apprenticed under Sailor Jerry in Honolulu, taking over his shop from 1973-99. He was an early proponent of tribal tattooing and created the modern version of the armband tattoo. He also standardized the look and packaging of tattoo "flash," the designs displayed on the walls of tattoo shops worldwide. Later, his Rollomatic and Sailor Jerry Bulldog Shaders were considered to be the finest custom tattoo machines made. He was, as he tried to explain the tattoo world to me, "a mayor at the national convention."

He was really more like visiting royalty from a foreign country. At my first tattoo conventions, it was easy to see he was one of the older (but not oldest) generation of tattooers and accorded a lot of respect. He never shilled himself, though, not like Lyle Tuttle or other peers. That modest streak cost him dearly, for many tattooers exhibited a carnival barker streak and bragged and buffaloed their way into magazines, honor dinners, awards, and other backslapping events. Going to a tattoo convention with Rollo meant a non-stop stream of grousing out of the side of his mouth. The best gossip occurred after our hotel room door shut at night.

Rollo's tattoo-inspired works also appeared at Chicago's Ann Nathan Gallery, the Bruce Bannatyne Gallery in L.A., and the Honolulu Academy of Art. The book *Bullseyes and Black Eyes* was a collection of his work and contained an extensive interview with him. He was also a die-hard collector of Oriental art, Japanese toys, and antique carnival chalk figures. Right up to the end, he lived like an overgrown little boy, surrounded in a mess of the things he loved.

After the initial crying jag was over—about two days—I dragged myself to my computer and started Googling Rollo. Someone paid for his Legacy.com page already and entries were accumulating.

Kandi and I spent a long time on the phone together, comforted in the odd bond we had—she was Rollo's girlfriend several years before me and a fellow tattoo artist. We swam the gamut of tearful emotions and finally tried making each other laugh about Rollo, which worked. Then she started filling me in about women who'd been in Rollo's life before and after me and were contacting her. There were long lists of them before me, reams of them, and a few afterward. Rollo, as Kandi reminded us during the memorial, was a womanizer.

Among the many declarations of love Rollo had made to me, the words, "You got me at a time in my life when I don't need to chase women any more," meant something. He'd confessed his many infidelities during his relationship with Kandi to me in detail and was genuinely apologetic. He'd been equally unfaithful to other women but the difference was he'd really loved Kandi and blown it with her. She'd booted him out of the relationship but they remained tattoo buddies, bonded in ink.

"I won't be that way with you," he promised. He kept the promise.

Still, there were lots of names in this conversation with Kandi. Many names I knew as old girlfriends of his who predated her. Some I had forgotten about. Others I was unaware of. Kandi had the job of going through Rollo's personal papers and she found old naked photos of yet another girlfriend of his. He must have hidden them at the tattoo shop because if I'd found them, I would have torched them long ago.

I looked up one name that Kandi mentioned on the Internet and was unsettled to see that she looked like me. *A lot* like me. It shouldn't have been such a surprise, for many of his women over the years resembled each other. He liked women with offbeat features and a few extra pounds, a preference that went back decades.

As I inspected the picture on my computer screen of this woman I'd never heard of but who apparently had a fling with Rollo after we split up, I was filled with jealousy. It came out of the green nowhere and turned to acid bile in my stomach. How dare she! How dare she…what? Enjoy time with a man I'd been married to for fifteen years? Respond to romantic overtures that had once been mine? I felt like an idiot for this jealousy, which was an unbelievably rotten feeling to experience amid fiery pain and emptiness and loss.

I tried to de-justify my raging emotions and clicked on his memorial page. Another former girlfriend had posted about their wonderful "romp." This name I knew because he'd taken up with her again while we were separated the first time. I'd found her name and phone number during a visit to Hawaii and seen where he'd written her name in tattoo lettering. *Fuck you, bitch! If he couldn't get it up with me, what business did he have trying to get it up with you?* I stewed and read on.

An entry from the daughter of his third wife galled me. He'd married wife number three within days of our 1999 divorce and I was really bitter about it. I secretly wished on the usurper all the pain and anger I'd gone through with him. That was unnecessary, as it turned out. Their marriage lasted about two years and was, as he told me in a letter afterward, "a mistake." I took more pleasure than I should have in knowing that his support payments to me outlived the third marriage.

The first wife popped up, too, with a boo-hoo note about how they'd been married too young. *Right,* I thought and tried to swallow a bitter knot in my throat, *is that why you cheated on him with his best friend?* He'd given her little thought over the years, at least while we were married. *Go back into the woodwork*, I privately ordered her. It seemed to work and I felt mildly better.

A few weeks later, I received notification of an entry posted on another site, this one that I had written the obituary for. It was from a girlfriend of his from the 60s, two decades before we met. I knew who she was because of a curious story he'd told me. In the 60s, Rollo made a decent living as a photographer, and it was on an assignment photographing tattoos that the flame was lit.

As his relationship with this old girlfriend was ending, he took a picture of her while she sat at the kitchen table crying. The next photo he took was of another woman, one who would become his next girlfriend, and in that photo she was laughing. Somehow, the negatives were double-exposed and he ended up with this accidental metaphor of love's fickle nature. I couldn't think of anything ill to wish on this ex-girlfriend because I felt sorry for her. Her grief didn't intrude on mine but I thought guiltily of the wife of my former lover and friend. Had I intruded on her grief? Yes.

Now I started to feel bad in a whole different way. I felt callow and small. I didn't mind sharing my horrific grief with Kandi at all. Very early on in our relationship, I told Rollo that we each had to name the one person in each of our lives that the other person would always have to live with too. I said Louis Black, my editor at the *Chronicle*. He said Kandi. She became my soul sister because we'd both loved the same man and his great artistic heart in the same way, only I got him at the better time.

And I felt like the grieving widow, despite that we'd been divorced eight years. I knew in my heart I was his true love, that of all his wives and girlfriends, I was The One. But I wasn't the grieving widow. I was the bereft ex-wife.

❧ ❧ ❧

After Rollo's death, I took my dog and ran away to the beach. When I returned, Corky—the friend who'd first introduced me to Rollo—and I decided to have a little farewell to the old man. We invited a couple dozen of the folks who'd known him and gathered on what would have been his sixty-fifth birthday.

I brought photos from over the years plus a few pieces of art. Corky brought his collection of *Honolulu Babylon*, a zine he and Rollo produced in the early 80s. It was wickedly funny, honed on the sword-sharp wit both possessed. On the cover of the third issue was a photo of Rollo holding a gun to his head, Corky's face right next to him. Macabre was the only word I could think of.

Rollo suffered from a variety of illnesses that finally encroached too much on his ability to live comfortably day-to-day. He always said he never wanted to linger with illness or be confined to a bed or become invalid. He told his tattoo partner Keith Underwood that if the diabetes got bad enough, he'd "suck a gun" before undergoing amputation. That phrase is so Rollo; it gave me shivers.

But not the cover of the *Honolulu Babylon*. "The Terminal Issue" it was called. Most people at the memorial looked horrified at it and then to me with pity. Not me. I just laughed. It was Rollo's black humor pulling aside the veil of death and reaching out to tweak me through the ether.

I will grieve for him the rest of my days.

AWARD-WINNING ROCK JOURNALIST MARGARET Moser is the author of three books, including *The Edge Guide to Austin* and *Rock Stars Do the Dumbest Things*, recently adapted for a VH1 program. A retired groupie and high school dropout with no college education, Moser directs the Austin Music Awards for South by Southwest annually. She is currently a senior editor and writer for *The Austin Chronicle*, has been a commentator on NPR, and written for Sony Records and *MOJO* magazine. She has five Chihuahuas and no tattoos.

Mollie McLean Staffa

Mortal Vexation

I WAS PISSED THE day my mother died. My psyche was burned from the previous sleepless nights, my bones were so, so weary from holding the rest of my family emotionally upright, and my head was completely nonplussed, unable to truly wrap itself around what had just happened. But that's not why I was pissed.

It didn't really have anything to do with the fact that there had been no meaningful conversation between my mother and me during this time, between the moment when the doctor told us it might be a week (but more likely days) and the moment when she died. There had been virtually no conversation at all. If hard-pressed to come up with the number of words my mother and I said to each other during those four days, I would make an educated guess and say twenty-seven. We just don't talk in our family. It makes us uncomfortable. We're Episcopalian, for God's sake. Suffering in silence is part of the credo they make you sign when you're confirmed.

I wasn't pissed that my mother's care while she was dying fell mostly at my feet. This was something I could do, something I was good at. I got it from her, so it felt natural and right, no matter how much I hated every second of it. I didn't get the versatile intellect that my sister and two brothers were blessed with. College was a rambling adventure to me, one I never treated seriously and undertook only because my father made it very clear there was no other option. Even after finally going back and getting my degree when I was in my thirties, I was still stuck in the same dead-end job I had been in before.

But somehow, I had always found the emotional reserve to deal with the worst situations life thrust upon me and those who were close to me: This was my gift. I never wavered because I had learned it from the pro. My mother was the emotional benefactress, as well as the office manager, of Saint James Episcopal Church. She should have been a priest. She worked for enough of them, doing nine-tenths of their jobs and giving them unconditional support. Never mind that it took up most of her time, and her own brood was left to fend for themselves when it came to making life-altering decisions. She made sure we were fed and clothed and that we were where we were supposed to be, but she was a social creature. Raising an increasingly moody family of independent children didn't fulfill this need. Her world expanded through the church, branching out into activities such as the local chorale and the community theatre, until she was rarely home in the evening. Retrospectively, I know she would have been there if she had ever been asked. It never occurred to me that maybe that was what she was waiting for.

We preferred nonverbal means of communicating emotion. Music was, and still is, a big one for my family. My father joined the Columbia House Record Club right after we moved to Texas. He let each of us choose one album of our own. My sister Jodi was the oldest. After careful deliberation, she selected Elton John's *Honky Chateau*. Jimmy, a year and half behind her, chose Three Dog Night's *Seven Separate Fools*. I picked the first thing I saw, The Partridge Family's *Shopping Bag*. My little brother Scott got *Simon and Garfunkel's Greatest Hits*.

Hindsight reminds me that this was a form of modeling. It was my dad saying: "This is what is important; this is what makes life good." To this day, I remember the four of us, circa 1976, fortunate enough to have our own rooms on the second level of our home, each playing individual copies of *Frampton Comes Alive* at the same time, always at different places on the record. I never remember my mother yelling at us for this, although I do remember my dad telling us to turn it down. But these were messages from them, a non-verbal legacy, investing and supporting this love of music within each of us, allowing us to explore and define our own tastes.

And yet we didn't have any music during those last two days of my mother's life to cover the vast chasm of words that were being thought, but not spoken. No music, save for the tinny sound of "Pachelbel's Canon," accompanied by waves crashing on a digital beach somewhere. A well-meaning friend brought this CD, thinking it appropriate, and put it on the inexpensive boom box that sat on the desk in my mother's room, letting it play over and over. The silence had been too much to bear, apparently, but this was somehow worse, associating this beautiful piece of music with the travesty that was being wreaked upon our lives. It was still playing in the background an hour after she died, and I feared I would feel nauseous every time I heard it from then on. But no, this was not what pissed me off.

My siblings and I did talk some during this time, but mainly about practical things—who was going to do what and when. I felt overwhelmed by what was happening, and the weight of what the next few hours would bring terrified me. I was irritated with my brothers and my sister; they acted as though it was natural, me being in charge, them looking the other way. But this was not natural; this was not usually the case.

The only real communication that occurred during this time came from my younger brother, Scott. The night before she died, my mother got up one last time; she wanted to sit in her living room. I got Scott up and he helped me move her into a chair. The air felt compressed, all of us restive, uneasy, unable to speak.

My brother pulled a piece of paper out of his pocket and announced that he had something to read, if our mother wanted to hear it. *Of course I do*, she said, although I remember she sounded so tired, and maybe not sure if she really wanted to hear what he was going to say. He began to read.

He thanked her for every thing he felt she had given him, for everything he felt made him who he was, what made life worthwhile. He thanked her for the subdivision that we grew up in and the freedom it provided us, the country club where he first joined the swim team, and all of the animals she'd let us have.

I lay on the couch in the dim light and I listened to him read this, feeling unsettled, kicking myself for not being able to do the same thing, wondering where in the hell he had come up with this idea. This wasn't how we did things in our family.

But now I realize this was how my mother did things; she was always reaching out. She reached out to those outside her family with open arms because they didn't resist her love. She reached out to us, her alienated scions, time and time again, with notes, refrigerator magnets, and stuffed animals none of us wanted. My home was filled with unappreciated messages of love, messages that were resented at the time they were given because they seemed an inadequate replacement. But I never threw them away; I somehow knew they were all I would be left with.

So listening to my brother extol on the virtues of the mother we had shared, I was filled with wonder, and shame. Why hadn't I thought of this? Because it never occurred to me, until now, until it was too late.

Yet, this wasn't what pissed me off.

She never really woke up again after we put her to bed that night. She tossed, she moaned; the hospice nurse told me she probably wasn't in pain; these were normal parts of the dying process. In the end, we watched as she succumbed the next day to a pulmonary edema, feeling helpless and wanting to do something, but knowing, finally, there was nothing else to do. Then she was gone.

My two brothers, my sister, and I all came together, our arms around each other, sobbing. All of the unspoken emotion gushed forth in this moment in which we were closer than we had ever been, clinging to each other, trying to find a place of safeness, together. We all held the best intentions, swearing we wouldn't lose this feeling, but I think we also knew that we would. It's just so much easier to go back to what you know.

We broke apart and started numbly talking about what to do next, haphazard in our movements and our thoughts. Scott looked down and saw George, my mother's cat, still lying close to her side, curled up in a ball, guarding her. He said he would take the cats. Jodi would deal with the financial end. Jim began calling the funeral home. They told me I had to get some sleep.

Within the hour, the grapevine had people at my mother's house with food, with love, with shoulders to lean on. The priest showed up and tried to start running things, telling me what I would do with my mother's body, and how the funeral would go. I had never liked nor trusted him. He always held me a bit too long and a tad too tightly when he hugged me, and I always felt a grope was just around the corner. But I had always smiled politely and wriggled away, not wanting to cause my mother any consternation. But she was gone. So I basically told him to fuck off and to get out of her house. He sputtered and protested and told me he knew what was best. I told him he really did not want to do this. He looked at my face, then left. Still, this wasn't it, as ready as I was to be mad at this man, as ferociously possessive as I felt of my mother at that moment; this wasn't what pissed me off.

They came and took her away, and I decided I was going home, just overnight. I needed a break; I needed my cats; I needed my own bed. No one wanted me to go; I hadn't slept in forty-eight hours, and it was a two and half hour drive. I remember feeling determined; the leftover adrenaline of my fight with the priest had me feeling better than I had in days. I felt like Scarlett begging Rhett to help her get home from Atlanta, even if he had to steal a horse. She had to get home to Tara, to her mother. Only her mother was dead. And so was mine.

I drove home, crying pretty much the whole way. It was the most wrong, most mind-numbing, hollow, aching feeling in the world. I was still thinking about Scarlett, and how she had cried when Melanie died, how Melanie asked her to take care of Beau, her little boy, and Rhett. Melanie told Scarlett how much Rhett needed her. It was lovely: the soft blurry light, in which Scarlett finally realizes how much Melanie meant to her, how she really had been like a mother, watching over her.

Then I thought about Emma and Aurora in *Terms of Endearment*. They epitomized the dysfunctional mother/daughter relationship, but they came together in that last sweet moment when Emma waved, then slipped away.

That's when it hit me.

I was possessed by a fury like I had never felt. I cried and raged at God and Hollywood for setting me up like this. All this time I had felt I was in a movie and everything was going to be nice and sweet and wrapped up in a box of popcorn, which would be neatly disposed of at the end, with closing credits and a soaring, heartwarming soundtrack to ease my mind. But it wasn't like that, not at all. I felt ravaged, because I knew death was not pretty. And most of all, I now knew it was permanent. It hadn't been so jarring when my father had died eight years before. He had been sick for a long time, and we felt his relief when he finally slipped away. And I had my mother there to comfort me.

But now she was gone. I realized I was closer to her than I had ever been during those last days, holding on to every last trace of her essence. I don't know what I expected, but not this. I would never have another chance to know her, to know who she was, what made her heart beat faster and kept her awake at night. I would never know what she dreamed of when she was a little girl, or why she never went to college. I had always meant to ask her why I have this scar under my chin, and if I actually saved that baby who fell into the pool when I was five.

All chances, all answers were gone, just like that, no warning. I have always resided in a world of unreality. I realized now that she lived in this world, too. She gave it to me. Like mother, like daughter.

We watched this movie of our lives pass before our eyes, allied in our unspoken resolve that it wasn't really happening, that my mother couldn't die. Because she was my mother.

Except she did. And I was pissed.

MOLLIE MCLEAN STAFFA IS the manager of a non-profit thrift store. She lives in Austin, Texas, with her husband and three cats. She is working on her first novel.

Lyman Grant

The Stuff of Dreams

"You do look, my son, in a mov'd sort
As if you were dismay'd; be cheerful, sir."
William Shakespeare, *The Tempest*

I HATE MOVING. FIRST, there are the books. I don't know how many, a few thousand, I guess. To me, a writer and English teacher, the quantity does not strike me as anything really totally outrageous, but it's enough that movers give me an unenthusiastic stare when we do the walk through for the bid. "Are *all* these going?" they ask. I say, "Yep," and spare them the story of my life, the interests, the hobbies, the career moves, the failed career moves, the fulfilled and unfulfilled dreams and desires that these books represent.

Next, there are the files: the marks-o-lotted boxes of correspondence, galleys, contracts, reviews, drafts of old works, drafts of abandoned—no, don't say abandoned—essays, poems, and books. I should stop, before I embarrass myself fully, but I need to mention the essays from graduate school, undergrad school, even high school memorabilia, including poems to many, many rose-lipped maidens by one heavy-footed lad.

And then there's the stuff that really puzzles my wife: my father's things, ratty Horatio Algers, textbooks, military training manuals, pennants from America's vacation destinations, baseball score cards from stadiums long demolished, brochures from historical sites, tax returns, and cancelled checks.

And, oh, I almost forgot. The record albums. The 33's. *Revolver*, *Sgt. Pepper's*, and Donovan's *For the Little Ones*—the first three albums I bought in '68 when my mother had cancer. Despite irregular culling over the years, six or seven hundred more still get boxed up and hauled around. There are yards of Jethro Tull, America, Poco, Zepplin, Mountain, Jackson Browne, Leonard Cohen, The Roches, John Lennon, Nancy Griffin, and Neil Young—well, CSNY in many forms, individually, paired, and grouped—Talking Heads, The Clash, Orchestral Maneuvers in the Dark, Men at Work, Laurie Anderson. One time period replacing another until CDs extend the obsession. Add the jazz and the classical to these and I have more music than I would want to listen to in a year. I even occasionally add to the collection—recently, McCartney's first solo record and Andy Griffith singing hymns.

So I hate moving, but this year I moved again. It was a good move, a needed move. Unlike Guy Clark's in "LA Freeway,"

Pack up all your dishes.
Make note of all good wishes.
Say goodbye to the landlord for me.
That son of a bitch has always bored me.

it was a move from the country, far from work and rising house values, into the city where gas and time are saved and equity grows. Still, it was moving.

Recently, therefore, I have been digging around the new garage going though all this stuff again because it won't fit in the new house. It didn't fit in the old house, either, and much of it was stored in the garage there also. Somehow, for nine years, I could never get around to dealing with it. But this time, in this new house, I have decided that we will park the cars in the garage and by the end of the year everything will be in the house or trashed, given away, or sold.

In the five months that we have lived in the new house, I have made sporadic progress. Still, piles of stuff rise to the ceiling. The brown boxes loom over me, like mounds of sandy loam, excavated and transported like the contents of graves, cardboard mini-caskets reading "U-Haul" and "Texas Fiction A-D" and "Study." With each box, over and over, it all becomes so apparent—the purity, the essence of my ridiculous life, the tenuousness by which I hold onto my self-esteem, the castles of stuff by which I fortress myself against the grief that is, at least, part of who I am. What grief? Why not let it all go?

Letting Go and the Comedy of Grief

Any discussion of grief, these days, must refer to Elizabeth Kübler-Ross's stages of grief: denial, anger, bargaining, depression, and acceptance. But other paradigms also exist. Roberta Temes describes three types of behavior displayed by those suffering from grief and loss: numbness, disorganization, and reorganization. Austin therapist Dan Jones has identified ten steps for closing a relationship, moving from denial to farewell and release. Even Dr. Phil has his own list of four stages: shock, denial, anger, and resolution.

As a teacher of literature, I am aware that each of these writers has identified a narrative, the plot of a story that people might use as a way to live. That story is structured upon what we lit-crit folks call a comedy, not funny-haha-comedy, but, simply, a story with a happy ending. Usually, in the first act of a comedy, life is fine, but suddenly it falls apart in some kind of conflict. Then there is chaos (exile, imprisonment, separation, just plain bad luck) and the dealing with that chaos (anger, bargaining, and depression). Finally, in the last act, the conflict is resolved, and life has a new purpose and is understood once again. In Shakespeare, for instance, we have all those weddings closing out the comedies, the coupling of opposites, new order, new beginnings, and all that.

As a structure for a life story, most of us prefer comedy against tragedy, which ends in death or at best hopelessness. I am even tempted to say that tragedies occur when a character has refused, or has been unable, to deal with grief, to move through the story that the stages of grief describe. I don't know if this theory will bear out with close analysis of dozens of tragedies, but it seems that the narrative of the tragic ending requires a character to hold on to negative emotions—fear, anger, revenge, hopelessness, guilt, shame, greed, you name it. Oedipus just can't forgive himself; Hamlet can't accept what has happened to his father. There is no "letting go" in *Hamlet.*

Conversely, the narrative of the happy ending requires that the character let go of various negative emotions and behaviors. As Dr. Phil says, "We've got to be accepting of those things we don't control." In other words, we must let go.

The odd thing for me is that I believe that I have let go of a great deal of negative history, and that's why all these possessions and the emotions they provoke surprise me so. The brief outline of my comedy is that my mother died when I was fifteen and left my father and me to fight about who was more angry. He said I would be a failure, and at the time, I didn't know enough to know he was wrong. In grad school, I was able to find a mentor who believed in me, and that saved me for a while. Then at thirty, I married a nice woman but the wrong woman, and together we had a wonderful son. As a college educator, I began moving up the administrative ladder. Together, my wife and I started a magazine, which became fairly successful. We bought our dream home. Then in a couple of years, my father, my mentor, and my father-in-law died; the magazine collapsed suddenly; I lost my administrative position at the college; and my wife and I separated. At forty-two, I had become a divorced dad in a one-bedroom apartment.

Luckily, in my mid-thirties I met John Lee and Dan Jones as they were founding the Austin Men's Center. With them, I learned to grieve various events in my life. Looking back, it seems that I spent my mid-thirties grieving my childhood and adolescence. Then I gave my forties to grieving my thirties. Since I have written about these events in various essays and poems, I will not say more about those years. All I should say is that therapy, friends, forgiveness, and love will get one through most of what life throws at you. Though it has taken time, I have rebuilt everything I lost a dozen years ago. Like I said, "my comedy"—I have married again, fathered two more wonderful sons, published more than ever, and worked my way back up the academic ladder. Happy ending, right?

Inside Out

Well, at just fifty-four, I am, I hope, a long way from the end of my story. And happy? I suppose I am happy, yet still I wonder why I have been so conflicted about all those books and records and files? I mean, seen from outside, doesn't it seem that a happy man has two options: 1) he either "lets go" of the stuff, moves on, moves in, and celebrates his simple life, or 2) he enjoys his stuff, brings it into the house, shelves it, stacks it, and rejoices in his abundant good fortune?

Of course, I am doing neither. At first, I stored a great deal of this stuff in the garage, and then like a man slowly going through psychotherapy, I allowed each box, box by box into the house. Until I allow it in, this stuff remains in the garage—a perfectly appropriate place to store those things about which I am ambivalent—that inside-the-house space that is still outside-the-house, the depository, the storage room, a kind of modern suburban cellar (the place for the submerged emotions and yucky things), but also a kind of transition zone, almost a porch with its great open yawning door, un-air-conditioned and un-heated, yet still enclosed on three sides, a kind of peninsula into the ocean of the world.

In *The Poetics of Space*, Gaston Bachelard writes, "Outside and inside form a dialectic of division, the obvious geometry of which blinds us as soon as we bring it into play in metaphorical domains. It has the sharpness of the dialectics of *yes* and *no*, which decides everything." I am tempted to assert that the stuff that I have brought into the house does not trouble me. I lifted it and carried it inside and have given it a place in my new house and in my new life. Once I bring a box inside, open it, and unpack it, its meaning, one might think, begins to transform from something that I don't know what to do with into something I know to be perfectly part of who I am.

For instance, in looking up the quote from Bachelard, I simply stood up from the keyboard, walked around my desk about five steps and pulled the book from the shelf where I knew it would be—with the other books of theory and poetics, arranged alphabetically by author's last name. Wouldn't one think, therefore, that this book by Bachelard produces less psychic troubles than the other books and papers in the garage? But Bachelard also warns of such simplistic notions—"Unless one is careful, it [the dialectic of inside and outside] is made into the basis of images that govern all thoughts of positive and negative."

In other words, we should be careful to protect ourselves against easy outside=bad and inside=good thinking. For example, among the first boxes to enter the house were those containing the albums. It was a practical decision; I didn't want to leave them in the scorching heat of the garage to warp and ruin. Many of these records are already thirty years old, and I don't want to replace them; perhaps many of them aren't worth replacing. Still, I have to admit that I am both proud and ashamed to own these records. So, the fact that these records are shelved in a music room does not mean that I reside with them easily.

First, they catalog the highlights of my pedestrian tastes. I am a middle-class boy, you know, with aspirations to become an intellectual. I know I could sell these records and pretend I am and was something other than what I am. I can deny that I ever yearningly sang "A Horse with No Name," and deny that still today I can whine the solo from "Whole Lotta Love." Conversely, I can sell these records and destroy the evidence that I did not have the good sense or taste to purchase *Are You Experienced* when it first appeared.

I think one way some of us survive growing old—one way that we forge ahead into a happy ending—is to outgrow any need to be "cool," to refuse any critical reconstruction of the past. ("If we loved the band America, by God, let's keep loving America. Let the critics and our own mature tastes be damned. 'Tin Man' is a great tune!") However, if we desire to remain "cool," we must perform our own critical reconstruction—package up our Chicago albums for Cheapo Discs and purchase every early Rolling Stones album we missed, no matter the cost, for prominent display in the den.

Second, my feelings toward my albums are a kind of grief, also, in that I did enjoy the 1960s and early 70s. I miss them, and I miss who I was then. I was filled with a joyful celebration of the genius of my generation, Rick Wakeman's concept album, *The Six Wives of Henry the Eighth*, Emerson Lake and Palmer playing Mussorgsky's *Pictures from an Exhibition*, The Who's *Tommy*, Nitty Gritty Dirt Band's uniting of rock and country with *Will the Circle Be Unbroken*. I was convinced that we could lift pop culture to high culture, that we would change the world, that peace and love would reign, that we would never sell out for money and security, for gourmet coffees and ice cream and tableware from The Pottery Barn. But I was wrong; and my album collection remains a record, unreconstructed and unrevised, of my indiscriminate romantic dreams. I wish I/we had been smarter; I wish I/we had been braver; I wish I/we had been geniuses and heroes.

Baggage, Souvenirs, and Trophies

So this is the method and my madness. The problem with all this stuff is not necessarily the quantity of it all. Sure, the sheer bulk provides me with a practical problem: Where do I put it all and how do I decide what enters the house and what doesn't? Still that problem is a problem with storage, not with meaning. The solution to the quantity problem is simply building more shelves, buying more file cabinets. It is a problem with an economical or architectural solution, not emotional ones.

So first, the albums entered the house—I had already built cases especially for them, decades ago, so they were easy to place. Next were groups of hardbacks, fairly expensive, mostly sets of American and British classics, all representing my bourgeois pretensions, and my dream to retire into a self-satisfied, disengaged, pre-modern Anglo reverie. They found their home in the living room, where, to be honest, guests can admire the cost, if not my taste.

Then, for a few months there was a pause and empty bookcases awaited in the study, while I considered which books to carry upstairs. After one false start, I settled on poetry and non-fiction. The choice came down to one question: In the next few years, what part of me do I hope to be nurturing; what part of me needs support? Since the next project I envision for myself is a book about Texas poets, I hunted for everything I owned concerning poetry, criticism, poetics, and literary theory.

Perhaps most liberating for me was that I unearthed a few boxes of books that can only be described as old-fashioned liberalism, books that were formative in my early desire to be a teacher, scholar, and writer. At the heart of these books is a certainty in the concepts of Truth, Beauty, and Goodness, once vibrant ideas, but now a bit desiccated, the residue of post-structuralism's dry breath upon them. I don't know when I packed up these books or why, but I had not seen them for a long time. Now, Joseph Wood Krutch has his place next to Julia Kristeva; Mark Van Doran leans over Raymond Williams and shakes hands with Slovoj Zizek. I had no idea how sweet it would be to unpack them.

Maybe I am feeling here the resolution of a grief peculiar only to the tail end of the boomer generation. But I perceive this grief of discontinuity throughout the nation. I think it is central to our country's cultural divide. I believe that at the heart of the Christian Right's political agenda is a grief over the loss of various "absolute" concepts like Truth, Beauty, and Goodness. For them, concepts such as "Family" and "Marriage" have been deconstructed beyond recognition. How does a person who loves tradition say goodbye to/let go of such beautiful ideas? Of course, denial, anger, depression will be part of the process.

On the other hand, the non-traditionalist left has to confront the choice of which "Family Values" it imports into its new family—mutual love and respect or power and violence, nurture or guilt and shame. My point is, for me, two married moms dancing in the living room to the Indigo Girls with their adopted children, laughing and dancing, is just as much a family as Ward, June, Wally, and the Beave. However, if a parent, any parent, becomes violent or neglectful, it's the same old shit, whether the child is in a traditional, patriarchal home or in some new configuration. As someone who has defended new definitions of "Family," I think we have either/or-ed ourselves into uncomfortable corners. Let's not celebrate or grieve the death of "The Traditional Family;" let's celebrate the strength and vitality of family love in all its manifestations, including the most traditional. I will no longer grieve over the exile of some of my once favorite, though old-fashioned, books and what they represent. I welcome them back home.

Mirrors and Memorials

My madness, therefore, is a response to the meaning of my stuff. Whether I confront my stuff in the garage or neatly shelved in the study, I still must deal with what it means to me. In fact, one reason that some of this stuff remains in the garage is that I can, for certain periods of time, forget that it exists. But there is always the stray weekend when schedule and inclination collide, and I step into the garage for things rightfully stored there—tools for a building project, machines for lawn work—and all hell breaks loose as I confront—as the therapists say—my unfinished business.

There is one thing that I have come to believe about grief. It is not solely the disappearance of the person that we mourn. We grieve, more painfully, the disappearance of ourselves in their eyes. They are the Other. As Freud, Kristeva, Lacan, and so many others on my bookshelves tell me, we know ourselves through others. Often we project on to them those parts of ourselves that we dislike. But we also depend upon them to see our beauty and magnificence, and in their perceptions, we see ourselves. When someone disappears from our life, a part of us disappears. Each death, each divorce, each lost friendship is a broken mirror. Perhaps worse, we toss that broken mirror into the buried time capsule of our memory. Over time, we live, we change, but they do not. Like Hamlet's father, the ghosts from our pasts roam asking for revenge or reconciliation.

When I confront the *Baseball Registers*, for instance, I really do not know, today, what my father would think of them or of me. All I have is some current fantasy based upon a severed relationship. The best I have is a wish for an acquiescent nod from the "baseless fabric of this vision"—as Shakespeare writes in his comedy *The Tempest*. I have the real memory of his saying, "If you sell my books, I will come back to haunt you," balanced with a Gestalt fantasy of his approval. So, the *Baseball Registers* and *Baseball Guides* will probably remain in the garage a while longer. I would like to see myself as a committed baseball fan, but I do not. If I find the space to bring them into the house, it will not be because they tell me something about myself or are part of my dreams for myself or for my sons. It will be because I found a little space in my present life to honor my father. It will be a memorial but not a statement of faith. They will tell me where I have been but not where I will be going.

❧ ❧ ❧

In a couple of months, the moving in will be complete, and I hope this particular trauma will be resolved. I will have unearthed, unboxed, all remaining artifacts of my past. The plan is simply this: Bring inside anything that sustains a dream; find storage for anything that records a dream accomplished; confront and discard anything that damages a dream.

I have, I hope, about twenty or thirty years left on this earth. Maybe this essay has merely been about this fact; I am no longer young. Some dreams have died and must be grieved and let go. Others must be nurtured and tended or they, too, will pass. And there are a few others that sustain me and give me hope. I have twenty or thirty years left. They may as well be happy years, unburdened by the accusations of things, filled instead with the stuff of dreams.

❧ ❧ ❧

LYMAN GRANT IS A writer who has worked at Austin Community College for almost thirty years. Currently, he serves as Dean of Arts and Humanities. An author or editor of six books, his latest, *The Road Home*, was published by Dalton Publishing. His poems, essays, and reviews have appeared in *Dallas Morning News, Texas Observer, Sulphur River, Creative Pulse, Texas Books in Review, Through the Fire, Literary Austin, Feeding the Crow,* and *Is This Forever, or What?* By the way, he recently built more book cases, and, now, all his father's books are in the house.

Gary Kent

Homage to the Broken Heart

WHY AM I WEEPING? I'm a tough guy, the kind of fellow that famed Texas writer Rolando Hinojosa would call an *hombre duro*—a "hard man." For over forty years I've made my living doing high-falls, rolling cars, riding bucking horses, being set on fire. I am a stuntman in motion pictures—too tough to tire, too mean to tame—yet, here I sit, tears spilling from my eyes like rainwater cascading off a weathered rooftop. Why? Maybe it's the sound of the music—"In the Arms of the Angels." It has been some time, now, since I have heard that mournful melody—lastly at the funeral of my much beloved wife, Tomi Barrett Kent. It was her request that the song be played as friends and family passed by her casket.

It is three in the afternoon, now. I am alone in the house—busily avoiding life—dodging feelings, memories, friends, by immersing myself in that grand illusion called television. The programming has been interrupted by the haunting voice of Sarah McLachlan singing the lyrics to *that* song. It is her plea for animal rescue, an endeavor I am committed to, and Sarah is surely prodding some slothful citizens into action. She is, however, also causing me to weep. It is just so sad, the sound—empty of all joy, all cheer, like a dirge. "This," I whisper to myself, "is as somber as it gets."

I have been engaging in this solitary, numbing TV ritual as a way to avoid continuing grief after Tomi's death. My wife loosed her earthly bounds some two years ago—yet, I still grieve if I succumb to reminiscence; if I recall certain memories or become acutely aware of the silence in my house, the absence of footsteps in the hall, the loss of a cacophonous clanking and clinking drifting from the kitchen.

Joan Didion refers to the first twelve months after losing a loved one as "The Year of Magical Thinking," a time one spends convinced that the departed one is coming back, that it has all been a dream gone terribly awry. In my case, the dream has turned into "the *years* of magical thinking." I cannot bear to rummage through, let alone dispose of, any of my wife's belongings. "After all, she will surely need them when she returns," I think.

I still anticipate Tomi standing on the front porch, waiting to greet me at day's end. Each night I imagine she is lying next to me in our bed—as always, warm and radiant, her head nestled into the pillow, hair falling about her shoulders like honey, flowing over gold.

My particular grief actually began, like a small migraine of the senses, when Tomi was diagnosed with cancer. It seemed at the time that she was just fine, a gorgeous sprite, dancing gracefully through my life like she had done for over thirty-three years. Suddenly, it all changed. The sprite began losing weight and assumed a grayish pallor that no amount of sunlight would correct. She tired easily. "I must be going through menopause a little early!" she joked; yet we both knew something more sinister was beginning to assault her body, undermining our usual conviction that we were both healthier than mangos and destined to live forever.

A first trip to the doctor for a check-up did not go well—much clucking of tongues and shaking of heads in grim unison. Tests were ordered, then more tests, more clucking, more heads bobbing. Deep in my psyche, I began to feel the ache, like a tooth in need of filling, only it was not a toothache, it was a precursor of dreadful news. We were presented the verdict, straight from the shoulder, matter of fact: "Lung cancer—fourth stage."

I felt like I had just been body-slammed by a water buffalo. I didn't look at Tomi—just slipped my arm around her, hugging her close. She wouldn't see any pity coming from me, no fear, no anxiety. I was going to be strong as a rock! The decision was immediate. "We are going to fight it...the disease, no matter what!" I stared at the doctor, confrontationally: "Get your shit together, 'cause we're gonna' beat this, dude!"

"How long?" Tomi's voice was soft, like a small child, praying.

"Well, the tumors are too far along for radiation or chemo. We'll try medication, but I would honestly say, maybe six months."

Whammo! The buffalo hit me again, only this time, I was prepared. I immediately stuffed the impact down into the bowels of my being where it would lie, unfelt and unacknowledged, for an eternity. Six months meant absolutely nothing to me. The next five minutes meant everything. Now, the plateau of right now, became a battlefield, and Tomi and I the warriors.

To my way of thinking, the toughest and most courageous people on the planet would have to be those quiet, hidden away folk (the no-see-ums), lying behind window shades and drawn drapes, suffering a long, painful illness that draws them closer and closer to certain death. After that comes the person (usually a husband, wife, son, or daughter) who is washing, wiping, feeding, holding, and hurting for his/her loved one as they embark on this frightening journey.

Some of you have been through, are going through, or will go through this seemingly simple but terribly complex, even supernatural, event. I know these things and can share them with you, as my wife and I fought a good fight against the ravages of lung cancer for nearly a year. Here, then, is a brief history of our experience:

Our house, from the outside, looked almost deserted—haunted, if you will. However, if you could have peeked through the keyhole, you would have seen love transcendent—strong love, removed from the vagaries of lust, vanity, self-indulgence. This was love on the edge. Two people alone, simply living for each other in the moment.

We noticed friends and relatives that used to visit frequently were gradually appearing only now and then, staying for shorter periods of time. Conversations became small talk, phone calls and email, a litany of prayer and platitude. "Y'all keep on fightin', hear?"

And what a fight it was. We built our own fortress, a special world, inhabited by muses, imaginary warriors, invisible advisors. We developed a deeper level of thoughts and ideas. We invented our own signals and secret gestures. There was a constant meeting of the eyes—words were unnecessary, and sometimes, in the way. There was much hand holding. (It hurts to be hugged when you are suffering from cancer.)

During the painful twilight of those months, we grew ever closer, more in love, so connected in body and spirit we were practically the same person. And we made a pact, Tomi and I, that no matter what: Love, respect, admiration, and gratitude would never be stolen from us by this ugly disease.

Sometimes, there was genuine, grab your sides and shake laughter. Like the time I took Tomi to Randall's market and placed her in one of those go-carts designed for the disabled. Tomi cranked that sucker up and took off like a teenager in a dune buggy. She was headed full throttle right for a stack of canned peas. "Stop, stop!" I yelled. "I don't know how to stop the damned thing!" Tomi yelled back, before screeching around the peas and disappearing down an aisle of breakfast cereals. I ran after her. Just before the produce department, she thought to turn off the key, and instead of crashing, came to a whimpering halt. Sighs of relief, much laughter, then we placed the vehicle in low gear and completed our shopping at a respectable pace.

There was the time in the kitchen when I spied a long column of ants moving toward the sugar bowl. "How did these get here?" I growled. Tap, tap, tap! (Tomi approaching on her walker)—"Hellooo, Einstein...*they crawled!*" (Tap, tap, tap, on into her bedroom.)

Tomi had always been beautiful, a natural blonde, lithe and graceful, an accomplished dancer in her time. Cancer tried to rob her of that beauty. Her weight shrunk from one eighteen to ninety-two pounds. Her high, prominent cheekbones were chiseled by the disease into thin lines, like knife wounds. One night, as I turned that frail body so I could more easily clean her (cancer victims, through the effects of treatment and medications, frequently lose the ability to control their bowels), I winced at her gaunt, skeletal appearance.

"How does that make you feel?" she asked. "That's the bottom you used to pinch and pat, now you've got to wipe it."

"It still looks pretty good to me, Babe." I gave her derriere a small pat, just to let her know the chauvinist was still around.

The night she passed, Tomi was lying in bed, on her back, watching *The Animal Planet* on TV. I was nearby, on the couch, returning phone calls, giving updates. Tomi waved her hand, a gesture that usually meant, "Come here, I need something." As I approached, I was struck again by her translucent beauty, by the absolute grace of her being. I leaned into her, "Would you like some water?"

"No," she whispered, "I just want you to know how much I love you."

I tucked the nightgown around her thin shoulders. "I love you, too, Babe, always and forever and then some."

I looked up at her face and suddenly she was gone, absent, her eyes wide open, her body already becoming board stiff. But, the strange thing was, in those lovely, almond eyes, she was smiling, staring straight ahead as though she had just caught a glimpse of something at once beautiful and powerful, welcoming her. I held her hand, I kissed her, and again, I did not feel the impact from the truck that had just slammed into me. I tucked my horror, my loss, my grief away—out of sight, out of mind. I am, after all, an *hombre duro*.

***

I was a brick, I am told, at the funeral. I don't remember it much, except for the guilt. Friends had arrived from California, Washington, New Mexico, New York. Four of our favorite stuntmen flew in to act as pallbearers, along with Ric Williams and Joe O'Connell, two of Tomi's favorite Texans. The flowers were plentiful, beautiful, spilling out into the foyer like spring bouquets overflowing an Easter basket.

I had arranged for David Zuniga, a Buddhist chaplain, to conduct the service. There would be no fire and brimstone, no talk of sin and repentance here. I gave a very nervous memorial speech, thanking my wife for all that she had taught me, reminded her how much she was loved and missed by family and friends. I promised to celebrate her every day of my life. I do not recall a lot of the ceremony. I was, as they say, in "cloud-cuckoo-land."

I do, however, remember that when I finished speaking and sat down, I was immediately enveloped in GUILT. Why did I not go to the coffin and speak to her directly, instead of addressing the audience? GUILT! Had I treated her well enough in life? Was I ever unkind? Mean spirited? GUILT! Was there more I could have done to help her? If I had just been stronger, more magic, more the hero, could I have saved her from death—kicked the ass of the grim one and sent *him* off to a lonely grave instead of my adored Tomi? GUILT! I stuffed the feeling away before it could overwhelm me. Banished forever, I thought, with the sorrow and the grief. I simply did not go to the coffin, I rationalized, because I did not believe she was there. In fact, I really did not believe that she was even dead.

I am not alone in this struggle with the acceptance of death. It has, I am sure, occurred since the human consciousness sparked to life eons ago, and whispered, "I am." For the first year or two, the years of magical thinking, I scarcely grieved. I avoided cleaning the house for the longest time. Emily Dickinson wrote, "The bustle in a house/The morning after death/Is the solemnest of industries/Enacted upon this earth,-/The sweeping up the heart,/And putting love away/We shall not want to use again/Until eternity." Mostly, I kept up a frenzy of activity, treating the mundane as though it was suddenly, somehow, very special.

I visited friends and family in other states, accepted a part in a play, attended my first school reunion. I showered affection on every animal I encountered, and tried my best *not to grieve.* She would not have wanted it, I assured myself.

Each human being, indeed all living things, grieve in their own way, in their own time. Lions at a watering hole, convinced a member of the pride is too old, too sick or injured to continue their trek, will gradually leave the afflicted one alone and move on. At the last, one lone lion remains by the side of the stricken one, attempting to encourage its doomed friend to join the journey. Eventually, even this solitary creature will slowly turn its back, tuck away the grief, and follow after the others—moving to a primal rhythm which informs it that life, in all of its beauty and travail, must continue.

Grief, however, that dark phantom clinging to the soul, does not disappear at the conclusion of a ceremony or the beginning of a journey. Ceremony and ritual may take care of, as the Irish say, "the necessaries." Grief, however, is another matter entirely. It does not respond well to pomp or circumstance.

For me, at last, there occurred a wondrous epiphany. I had not, since Tomi's death, availed myself of grief counseling. I preferred to suck it up and face it alone. Tomi had been so strong, seldom complaining about pain or giving in to what must have been a wagonload of fear. "If she could handle it, I can handle it," I said.

Her illness and the way she dealt with it became my benchmark. Then, out of the blue haze of serendipity, an event occurred that changed my dealings with grief forever. I was invited by Hospice Austin to attend a memorial for all of those who had recently passed on. It would be a gathering of loved ones honoring family and friends no longer here. I decided to attend.

As expected, the memorial was held in a large, cavernous cathedral, at once intimidating and impersonal. The seats were filled to capacity with shadowy, silent mourners. A theologian of some renown gave a long, sonorous presentation, extolling the mystery of life, the relief that surely must arrive with death. At the conclusion, she invited members of the audience who wanted to say a word about their particular loss to approach the podium and have at it. At first, no one responded. Then a young girl, sobbing most uncontrollably, staggered to the stage and began to talk. She had just lost her mother and the hurt and the unfairness dogged her. I admired her for having the courage to share her feelings. I wanted to hear her story, but she was crying so heavily her words were incoherent. She concluded and returned to her seat. No one applauded. No one volunteered to be next. No one, that is, but me.

I decided to take the stage and celebrate Tomi, something I had promised to do at her funeral two long years ago. I hadn't a clue what I was going to say, or even how to begin, but I started in talking about Tomi's love for animals and her successful efforts in animal rescue, a subject I had forgotten to mention in my funeral address.

As I related tales of her derring-do, I heard laughter begin to sift through the audience. It was at once joyous and contagious. I opened my heart, unlocked private doors, threw up the sash of cobwebbed windows in my soul—immediately I felt Tomi's spirit spring free, like glorious sunshine flooding into a house of darkness.

I regaled the crowd with further tales of her adventures—the time she had a rock group on their hands and knees, crawling through the Johnson grass, over fire-ant mounds, feverishly pursuing a terrified kitten or rancorous canine in hopes of a rescue; and the time she and her gorgeous, six-foot tall model friend, Simone, journeyed late at night to the worst part of town to nab an abandoned feline. The poor creature was about to be a mother and was too sick to care for herself, let alone a family. They put her up at the Kent manse, and nursed her back to health just in time. It was Christmas; they named her Merry, and Merry gave birth to a healthy litter of nine kittens. Tomi and Simone found them all loving homes. Merry was adopted by our neighbors, whose son adores her, and shares his bed with her and sings her to sleep at night.

When I finished my frenetic storytelling, the audience burst into applause. Inappropriate? Who cares. The first person to approach me after the talk was a large, black woman. She wanted the address of Tomi's organization, as she wanted to make a donation. Then a tiny, middle-aged Asian man gave me a timorous embrace. Smiling, he informed me that this was the first time he had laughed since his wife died. *And I could feel Tomi's spirit, illuminating all of us in a soft, warm glow.* Later that night, in reflection, I realized that, in my case, my grief was actually much like a scar. If visible on the outside, where others can witness it, grief can be healing and beautiful, like flower therapy.

❧ ❧ ❧

This brings me full circle to my sitting in the chair, weeping at the sound of McLachlan's "In the Arms of the Angels." Have I learned anything at all in regard to the grieving process? Yes, I have. My humble advice then to others who keep the spirit of loved ones and lost treasures buried away, out of sight and mind, is to *bring them forth—set them free.* As Friedrich Nietzsche mused, "Out of the very love one bears to life, one should wish death to be free, neither a matter of chance or surprise." Do not go on a guilt trip! Take a trip to Paris, maybe, Pomona or Paducah, but do not take a guilt trip! Lastly, be thankful to your departed one for having had the grace to love you and to yourself for having had the courage to accept that love.

GARY KENT STUDIED JOURNALISM at the University of Washington. After duty in the Naval Air Corps, and writing publicity for the crack flying team, The Blue Angels, Kent started a theatrical career with the famed Alley Theater in Houston. In Los Angeles, Kent carved out a career in motion pictures as screenwriter, director, actor, and stuntman. His film, *The Pyramid*, took First Place, Docu-Drama, at the USA Film Festival (now Sundance), and his drama, *Rainy Day Friends*, won Best Special Stunt in a Motion Picture at the International Stuntman Awards. Kent's writing has been published in *Runner's World*, *New Texas*, and *Conversations with Texas Writers*, UT Press 2005. His book *Shadows and Light: Journeys With Outlaws in Revolutionary Hollywood* will be released by Dalton Publishing in May 2009.

Mylène Dressler

Flying Dutchman

THE YEAR WE TAUGHT a Tzotzil Indian how to ride a bike in exchange for his homegrown lettuces was the year my father died. That was the year of the soot-covered dog lying in front of her burned-out home, waiting for owners who never came back to reclaim their ruined possessions. That was the year Oliver Stone came to town and strolled with masked Zapatista rebels through the streets; the year my husband's bus was hijacked by demonstrating farm workers, who rode with him in silence all the way back up into the mountains, all of them watching a Jean-Claude Van Damme video together on the in-cab TV. It was the winter we had to burn a fire night and day to keep warm; the year of the big social justice conference; the year the mule coming off the mountain nearly ripped my arm off; the year my mother went alone to scatter my father's ashes on the North Sea. It was windy, and once dropped, my father's dust churned into clouds of gray suspended matter on brown water—I saw this on the video my mother sent me.

For months before that year, that year of the bicycle lessons and the runaway mule, my father had followed with eagerness and excitement my plans to become an expatriate in deep southern Mexico. An old-fashioned, dapper, fifty-five-year-old European who'd sailed the world widely and lived in many countries, he couldn't wait to see how my tender, American-reared soul would adjust to the remoteness of highland Chiapas, to the tenor of mountain life, the strangeness of local customs, the noise, the quiet, the cold, the heat, the poverty, and the wealth sitting squarely on top; the inability to get much of anything in the exact form that you wanted it, when you wanted it; the cleanness behind the dirt, and the dirt behind the cleanness; and the being cut off from most of the rest of the world. It was the year, almost the exact year, before cell phones and everyone getting email. My father had recently learned Windows, and on the rudimentary Internet he could check his stock quotes, but not much else. Don't worry, Dad, I'm going to share everything that happens with you, I'd told him. I'll call once a month, and we'll write often. He was reassured, briefly, but then—don't trust the postal services down there, he'd added, or what you send will never get through. You'll have to find another way, DHL, something. And be sure you have access to good medical care, Mylène. That part's extremely important.

He spoke from experience: His third heart attack had felled him in a tiny village in eastern Java, and as he lay on the bed above a swept dirt floor, with a crude IV nailed to him, black chickens had pecked at his window sill. The last attack, the one that really got him and started the long, uncertain road to the end, took him by surprise in Brussels, Belgium. The Flemish doctor there said it was quite simple: He could have a transplant or be dead in five years. But my father didn't want a transplant. He said he wanted to ride it out with the heart he had. He was a widely traveled man, but the thought of a foreign heart inside him was simply more than he could bear.

The bicycle was a sturdy Chinese model my husband had bought for a thousand pesos so he could ride in his spare time over the rugged hills and the cobblestones. Because he knew we couldn't take it back to the States with us when my writing fellowship expired, he started thinking, early on, about what he ought to do with it, about who might get some really good use out of it, once we were gone. Our gardener, Xalik, was a sharply wrinkled man who every day hiked many miles from his home village to reach the house we'd rented. His job was to build a simple, stone-bordered bed in the courtyard before the house's owners, American anthropologists, got back from the Pacific Northwest. He showed us the sketch they'd drawn for him before they left—but from what we could tell, he wasn't too concerned about following it. He spoke enough Spanish to wink and smile at us. Sometimes, at the beginning of the week, he asked to borrow money, for reasons he didn't explain; he always paid us back by the end of the same week, accompanied by interest in the form of his lettuces.

During the day my husband taught Xalik to ride, and I climbed into the cupola of that house and wrote. From my watchtower on that cold March morning, I could see not only the cobbled streets below, where the bike bounced and Xalik struggled along on a frame that was two sizes too big for him, but the larger cobbles of the foothills, blue in the distance. The nearest mountain to us had nothing human on it, other than a small church at its peak. That bare hillside suggested openness to me, breathing room in this part of the country so overwhelmed by displaced farmers and rootless settlers. I didn't know the mountain's name. All I knew was that on the day my mother had picked for pouring my father's ashes into the sea, I needed to be up somewhere high. The ritual, in fact, was already set in my mind. I would take flowers and a letter and some kindling.

I think it was only because I knew exactly what I *was* going to do on that day looming ahead that I managed not to go insane in the belfry of that house, not being able to tell my father about the mountain and the lettuces and the ever more wildly inventive garden border and the way the chimney smoked whenever the wind came from the north.

I calculated the time difference between Rotterdam and San Cristóbal and telephoned my mother I would be on that mountain at the same time she was at her dock by the sea. She and I slept in the same bed the night my father died, not wanting it to be so empty for her. We arranged, together, the memorial service for our family and friends, played my father's favorite music, ate his favorite foods, put out his pictures and his books. Then my mother had sent me on to the mountains. The rest, for her, my brother, and me, would be private.

Near the bottom of Calle Comitán, our steep street, past the blackened, lonely dog, was a flower market, and it was here we stopped for traditional lilies and gladiolus. It took us a while, getting lost a few times, to wend our way through the alleys and the low, tightly packed houses, to find the bottom of the mountain, where a dirt path clearly led to its summit. That early, so early some of the church bells were still ringing, no one seemed to be either going up or coming down. We went on with our bunches.

We passed a stray dog that, typically, slunk away from us with its tail between its legs. Our street's sooty, blackened mutt hadn't allowed us to get near it that morning, either, and that was also typical. We left it food, anyway, at a safe distance, and always made sure it had enough water. It was a slight, silent animal. We never once during that year heard it whimper or complain. The house it belonged to had been reduced to rubble. No one came back and no one was going to. There were far too many other burdens and preoccupations that winter. I'd been told by my worried governmental hosts that I must understand I would run some risk if I talked to any of the masked rebels or took part in any street protests. At the social justice conference, human rights were being discussed, but most foreigners weren't allowed or invited to sit in.

My father probably would have roundly seconded the *just-stay-out-of-it* advice. He never once voted in an election that I knew of. Although his passport was European, he knew no continental allegiance. He was simply always ready to go wherever he was required, or where his interests took him, and adapted to whatever milieu he found himself in—at least, outwardly. Inwardly he was often lonely, I know, and independent to the point of isolation. If he didn't trust his local employees to help him do the work, then he did the work himself. If he didn't believe his local suppliers were being honest, then he went down to the docks and counted the shipping containers himself. If one of his tanker vessels sailed straight into a typhoon, then he stayed up all night in a bar with his Scotch and personally chain-smoked it into port. He wasn't very good, he would have allowed, either at delegation or at faith.

He should be buried at sea. My brother and I agreed with my mother on that. There was nowhere else fitting we could think of.

The tiny white church at the crest of the mountain wasn't much more than a dome and a door, and locked and deserted. I passed it undeterred. Scrappy green grass covered the rest of the small summit and patches of bare, red dirt. We were high enough now that we could see over everything, over all of San Cristóbal de las Casas, and although it was overcast, the colors of the town still seemed bright, the way things tend to be at high altitude.

I lay the lilies and gladiolus in the shape of a square in the dirt. Then, inside this geometry, my husband prepared and lit the tinder we'd brought from our fireplace. When the small blaze was glowing and snapping, white smoke rising into the gray sky, I reached into my pocket and pulled out a letter I'd written only the day before, telling my father how he was missed. There was no wind, I remember. The plume went straight up. Shot like an arrow. I cried and then sat quietly back. We rested and noticed there were other dirt tracks that went across and descended the mountain in different directions—but decided that when the time came we should go home the same way we'd come. Later, when my long letter was completely burned, and the fire could be safely stamped out, we left the flowers where they were, and turned away. In my mind, those gladioluses are still there.

The mule bolted from somewhere behind us, crossing over from another path. Not knowing any better, and still a little blurry, I reacted foolishly when I understood what was happening. I heard someone shouting at us to stop it. So I stopped and put my hand out to the pounding animal coming down the path, at full speed, ears locked, eyes steady. In less than an instant I felt the slam, the hook, and a tearing weight and force—but somehow got untangled from the bridle just as my body was about to be dragged down the hill with it. A young man raced by us helplessly.

The place where Xalik finally learned to ride, my husband came home and reported to me one day, was out near the edge of town, on a long, rectangular, grassy strip of field. All along he'd been worried that the steep hills, along with the uneven cobbles, would make it difficult for Xalik ever to learn to balance properly. Yet whenever the two of them had gone together to one of the flat *zócalos*, or squares, they were driven off by drunken, unemployed young men who lunged at the handlebars in boredom. Freed suddenly from the worry of unhappy workers snatching at him, and of falling on the gleaming cobblestones, Xalik was able to cut loose, and fly, his arms bent, his neck steady, his toes alone reaching but keeping constant contact with the pedals. My husband gave him the bike that summer, and we were inundated with lettuces, and now beans. I couldn't speak Tzotzil, so I had no language, really, in which I could tell Xalik about what it meant to me, to see him riding that Chinese bike, or about the mule, and my father, the little Dutch kid who'd learned to ride before he ever set sail.

❧ ❧ ❧

MYLÈNE DRESSLER WAS BORN in The Hague, the Netherlands and is the author of three novels: *The Deadwood Beatle*, *The Floodmakers*, and *The Medusa Tree*. She lives and writes in the canyon country of southern Utah, where she is at work on her fourth novel, *The Wedding of Anne Frank*. Her father, Carl Martin Kalhorn, died in 1995 at the age of fifty-five.

Anonymous

An Anger with Many Names

OCCASIONALLY, I GET ONLINE and try to find people from my past. Only occasionally, because I usually find them in the obituaries and then I remember why it had been so long since last I tried. And then, I remember what it does to me. How it reminds me. How it stirs the anger. My anger. My grief. Not anger at the people who have died, but anger at the disease that killed them. A disease insidious, cunning, baffling, powerful. Yes, *that* one: the disease of addiction.

Of the thirty-one people in my graduating class, seven (that I know of) have died as a direct result of drugs or alcohol—three of them before the age of twenty-five. Staggering odds, but not if you know that I am from Alaska. Land of the Midnight Sun. Land of the highest rate of alcoholism per capita in the world, save Russia.

Each time I hear of another of these deaths, I relive all the rest. Intellectually, I know that brains do this—searching for a way to associate the experience. But, like a past depressive episode, I forget just how deep it can take me until I am too far in to go back.

First I cry. Then I yell. Then I sob. Then, I find myself singing an ancient Tlingit song I only seem to remember in those moments, curled in a fetal position, rocking myself like a child. It seems to be the only song that soothes and I don't even remember what it means.

I have been clean and sober for many years, have helped countless people get there as well—and watched countless fail. One would think that after so many failures, I would have stopped caring. Stopped trying. But I can't. The disease is my nemesis. When I see its grip upon someone, I attack. And it breaks my heart, deeply breaks my heart, every time I lose a battle.

I never forget their battles, I never forget their names, I never forget their ages, and I never forget what killed them...

Gunshot to the head, Bradley, 19
Overdose, Kris, 24
Boating accident, Jonathan, 22
Car accident, Shawn, 16
Liver disease, Auntie, 54
Plane accident, Danny, 34
Overdose, McClain, 23
Overdose, David, 32
Jumped off bridge, Darcy, 42
Plane accident, John, 29
Liver disease, Jenny, 40
Liver disease, Ronald, 42
Overdose, Travis, 26
Car accident, Scott, 27
Overdose, Sarah, 17
Hep C, Andy, 30
Hep C, Paul, 43
Car accident, John, 45
Slit wrists, Emma, 25
Car exhaust, Shirley, 41
Car accident, Jenny, 36
Knife fight, Thomas, 24
Cancer, my father, 73.

When I first got sober I would occasionally show up for family get-togethers. My father would always say to me, Crown Royal on the rocks in his hand, "So, still not drinking, eh?"

"That's right, Dad," I would respond. "It has been X months/ years now."

He would shrug and take another drink.

Years later, after being diagnosed with emphysema, prostate cancer, liver disease, and finally, the esophageal cancer that killed him, he sat opposite me in a hospital cafeteria, and said, "So, you still not drinking, eh?"

"That's right, Dad," I said, choking back tears. "It has been seven years now."

"Good," he said and looked away.

Sadly, that was the closest moment I ever shared with my father.

Grieving a loved one who has died as a result of addiction or suicide is a special battle. Anger is not a stage of its own in this particular grief. It is an overwhelming emotion present at every stage. After all, how could they do such a thing to the ones they claim to love and care about? The answer is in the sad truth that while they are in the throes of their addiction addicts are incapable of thinking of others. To quote the big book of Alcoholics Anonymous: "Selfishness—self-centered-ness! That, we think, is the root of our troubles. Driven by a hundred forms of fear, self-delusion, self-seeking, and self-pity, we step on the toes of our fellows and they retaliate." And so it is.

During these times of loss, I can find comfort in the company of other addicts—the fellowship and universality found in twelve-step programs can be a powerful healing tool. For those who do not have such an understanding support group, however, recovering from this kind of loss can be a painful and lonely place.

I find it particularly difficult to comfort non-addicts who have lost their loved ones to the disease of addiction. Just how do you tell someone that they were likely the last thing on the person's mind? That the insidiousness of a disease that tells its sufferer they don't have a disease is the real culprit? I have found it wise to hold fast to my anonymity in these circumstances if I can. I imagine it is not very comforting to be face to face with what likely resembles the actual personification of one's grief.

This is a poem I wrote for a colleague who tearfully shared with me that her stepmother had just died of an overdose.

DEMONS

I did not know you
but I did
At least I know our demons
shared a similar name

My anonymity holds fast
as I watch from the outside
your demon reap his wreckage
on those you left behind

In her eyes I see the tears
that could easily have been his
falling in a senseless puddle
beside his mother's grave

On her lips I see looming
the baffling question "why"
On her mind I hear thoughts
of things she could have done

My heart so wants to tell her
that the answers are never clear
That your actions do not undo
the love you had for her

My anonymity holds fast
as I fight my own tears off
for a comrade now in the arms
of whatever your power be

I did not know you
but I did
At least I know our demons
shared a similar name

I did not share this with her until several years after her loss. And she confirmed for me what I had already suspected: If I had shared the truth with her at the time—that I was a recovering addict—she probably would have seen me as a conspirator of sorts. That her anger at the time was large enough to engulf every addict in the world—to strip them of all of their rationalizations, smother every clumsy justification, and drown every hint of trying to blame their behavior on that damned "disease."

And justifiably so: Her anger at the addict is as strong as mine for the disease itself.

Buffy Cram

Still Life with Loss

IN MY FAMILY, APRIL Fool's Day was never a time for pranks or laughter of any kind. If it fell on a weekend, it was the one day of the year my mom and stepdad's bedroom door stayed closed all day long. My brother and I didn't know what exactly went on behind that door except that a lot of cigarettes were smoked and a lot of soft murmuring could be heard. Meanwhile, on our side of the door, we got away with wearing pajamas all day and watching too much TV. My stepdad would emerge from the room once or twice, red-eyed, grumpy, to use the bathroom or to get a glass of water. At some point my mom would tiptoe into the kitchen to make us food. We would speak in whispers while we ate our somber meal, the three of us orbiting around my stepdad's grief like it was our own.

If April Fool's Day fell on a school day, my brother and I would find ourselves standing straight-faced in the background while our friends smeared glue stick on the teacher's seat or slipped fake notices into her stack of morning announcements. We watched but were unable to take part because that would've been a betrayal of the grieving we knew was going on at home. I remember wishing there was some way to warn my friends that more than any other day of the year, April Fool's tempted people to do desperate and awful things, things that could poison a whole family, seeping down through the generations.

Instead, I ended up criticizing, telling them it wasn't even a *real* holiday and that their pranks were stupid—without really understanding the connection between their kind of pranks and the kind I'd been warned about at home.

After being away from his wife and kids for many weeks, drinking and gambling and who knows what else, my stepdad's father pulled into the driveway early on the morning of April 1, 1956. My stepdad and his siblings were seated around the table eating breakfast when their mom called out, "Your father's home." They pushed their chairs back and raced into the living room to stand by their mother. The kids waved, squealed, jumped up and down, but their father didn't move from behind the wheel. The four kids and their mother lined up inside the large picture window must have looked like the final family portrait. He just stared up at that living room window with a strange look on his face for a moment, and then twisted around to pick something up from below the passenger seat. When he came back into view with the rifle in his mouth, my stepdad's mom tried to shield as many eyes as she could. "Close your eyes!" she screamed. "Turn around. Close your eyes!" But there were too many eyes to shield. It all happened too fast. Forever, my stepdad would recall the way his father's mouth twitched around the barrel of the hunting rifle. Forever he would be able to envision blood and brains all over the back and side windows of his father's Barracuda, the body slumped forward over the steering wheel, horn blaring, neighbors starting to cluster at the end of the driveway.

What I know about loss I learned early and by example, from watching my stepdad cycle through his yearly calendar of losses, from the anniversary of his father's burial later in April right through to the last time his father's Barracuda pulled out of the driveway at the opposite end of the year. In between those dates were a whole slew of other anniversaries marking more recent occasions for grief. There was the day my mom's dad died, the deaths of different house pets we'd had, the day my stepdad lost his job, the day a friend of theirs drowned on a fishing trip, the day our house burnt down, the day of the car accident that nearly killed my mom and stepdad, although I never could figure out if we were grieving the near miss of the accident itself or the loss of the prized truck that crumpled like a tin can against a rock wall at forty miles per hour.

I learned that as people live their lives, they accumulate loss until, by the time they are adults, their year is crowded with it. I learned that loss can descend on a life, dividing it without warning into the severe categories of *before* and *after*, *then* and *now*. I knew the way the mind staggered after such loss, unable to comprehend its permanence, and how loss made people cling to "before," suddenly unable to do the most basic subtraction, unable to accept a void where once there was someone, something. I myself had struggled to accept the pile of charred wood, ash, and debris where our home had once stood. I'd cried over the row of empty food dishes out our backdoor, where our cats, Sushi, Scooter, and Jedi had once eaten each morning. I knew it was important to become skilled at loss, to let it have its way with you. Like my stepdad, I vowed that I would become a librarian of loss. I, too, would clear a space inside me where loss could stack up against loss in neat and tidy rows. I would tend to my losses, sorting and storing them for easy access, pulling them out once a year on their anniversary to hold them up to the light and say, *Look what nearly ruined me*. I learned all of this without having experienced too many losses of my own. Those were yet to come.

When they did come, my own losses were sloppy and impossible to file away compared to my stepdad's. I rarely had the finality of death. Instead, the people I lost were pulled away from me incrementally, by addiction or mental illness or both, and so my grief was open-ended, a Mothers-of-the-Disappeared kind of grief—hope and loss mixing together to make a kind of emotional papier-mâché. My grief asked me to accept that the people I'd lost were both *here* and *not here*, that they were standing before me but out of reach. I had to constantly remind myself that the people I loved were not who they said they were, not how they used to be. I knew that this kind of grief had a way of hardening around a person, hollowing her out until eventually she was no longer herself, but a statue of her grief.

I'd say my losses started with my high school friend Donovan. In the final years of high school he became addicted to cocaine and, eventually, heroin. He stole from me, lied to me, and broke into my family's house. I was with him when he ran full-force into the plate glass doors of a hotel lobby, when he had his first drug-induced heart attack, and when he was arrested his first and second and third times. I was there when, eventually, all of the people who loved Donovan had to cut him off. What surprises me about this grief has nothing to do with the violence he exposed me to. It has nothing to do with the residue of guilt that comes from having given up on a person. What surprises me is how my grieving for Donovan has kept pace with my life all these years. I'll be on my way to school or work, living in a different city, on a different continent, and suddenly I'll see my surroundings through Donovan's eyes. I'll know with assurance that he would appreciate the way the light slides out from under the heavy clouds, or this song, this glass of wine, this meal. In liminal moments before or after sleep, I'll remember the time he dragged me out of the house during the biggest blizzard my hometown had ever seen, how the entire city was ours that night, how we clambered over ten-foot snow drifts and lay on our backs in that changed landscape drinking red wine, thinking up futures for each other. I have recurring dreams where he's tricking me, leading me down dark alleys or into even darker woods. I chase after him and he disappears ahead of me. He's always slightly younger than when I knew him, healthier, the air around him bright and alive. When I finally catch up to Donovan, I find he's made of tissue paper, and then, of course, it starts to rain, each drop taking a bite out of him, dissolving him. Sometimes I try to fold this paper Donovan up and slip him in my pocket, but he always rips. One way or another, he comes apart in my hands. The dream is desperate, filled with an urgency beyond questioning. It's only after waking that I wonder, *Why this friend? Why this particular loss?*

The last time I saw Donovan he was emaciated, living on the street outside the needle exchange in Vancouver. I stopped to look at him, noticing how much older he seemed, the way his skin hung loose off his bones. He glanced towards me, but his eyes skipped past, lusting after too many other things to rest for long on the face of an old friend. I wasn't sure if he didn't see me or just didn't want to, but I hoped my having seen him would finally put an end to the dreams. What I didn't understand then is that the real-life Donovan had little to do with the Donovan living in my mind. That Donovan, the one that is a part of me, has become an archetype, a stand-in for every other type of loss. I imagine a totem pole, one loss standing on the shoulders of another, rising out of the dark and unreachable parts of my mind. It's Donovan who tops my totem of loss, Donovan who comes to me in my dreams because the other losses, the ones stacked up beneath him, are too difficult to face.

In my early twenties I called a certain amount of loss and grief into my life through the people I chose to date. It seemed I was only interested in men who had a special talent for being able to turn into someone else overnight. Their retreats were always sudden, like the peel-back of a wave, leaving me beached and alone with what seemed an unbearable sadness. At times it felt as if my losses were stinging me from all angles, as if they were conspiring with the hundreds of thousands of details that made up my days. I was astounded, almost flattened by the grief that lay waiting in ordinary objects. That pen, that photograph, this key chain: Each one was a sudden reminder of the person I'd lost. There were days when I'd see my loss standing on every street corner, a certain tilt of the head, a gesture or a particular color of eye—that same blue or green or brown I swore was so unique—blinking back at me, everywhere. For a while it seemed the whole world was built upon my sorrow, that it had somehow bled out into the world, that I myself was bleeding out, and then, one day, against all expectations, my grief would lift off, as light as old skin, and underneath it, I'd find I was new again. It's only now, at the end of my twenties that I can see why this loss of love hurt so badly, that, like the Donovan dream, it was one thing disguised as another. My grief wasn't about the boyfriends as much as it was about everything else. In the partners I chose, I was searching for an arena to act out loss again and again, hoping each time I would somehow get my other, deeper losses right.

You hear about people losing their entire families overnight. You hear about car wrecks and plane crashes, house fires and carbon monoxide poisoning. It's almost impossible to imagine grief of this magnitude. You wonder how anyone can live through such a sudden rearrangement of facts. By the time I was twenty-two, I had lost my family, but it wasn't sudden and it didn't involve accidents. It was a more drawn-out process—a slow dissolve, like tissue paper in the rain.

I lost my mother once, twice, a third time to alcoholism. Three times she turned to liquid before me. I tried to cup her in my hands, to run her to safety without losing a drop, but always she spilled over, slipped through my fingers, parts of her lost forever. Three times she returned to me—renovated, clear, rising to new heights of motherhood. For a while we would be more than mother and daughter. We would be like shipmates, survivors, savoring each moment we had as only the truly starved will do. And then she would drift away again, her need as inevitable as the tides and I would feel all of me curling around the emptiness inside me, stiffening around what I could not change or accept. I felt it happening to me—I was slowly becoming a statue of my own grief.

I lost my stepdad to mental illness. Looking back, I see that he was always on a slippery descent. There were times when he believed he had secret powers, that the world was full of magic omens. As a child it was wonderful to believe in him. After all, his powers didn't seem any more far-fetched than Santa Claus or the stories my mother read to me from the *Ladybird Children's Bible* each night. As I grew older though, my stepdad started to develop a savior complex. He started to believe, in earnest, that he was Jesus Christ. Before long he was locked into that narrative of persecution and crucifixion and everyone, including my mom, my brother, and I, became his enemies. He was being tugged at from below, pulled down to a place we couldn't follow. From time to time he would bob up for air making apologies and promises. He'd admit he was afraid, that things weren't making sense. He would agree to get help and we would all keep hope. But over the course of seven years, he was dragged completely under. Although he looked much the same on the outside, the person we had known, the person who had taught me so much about loss, had disappeared.

By the time I set out on my own, I'd had enough of loss. I'd had a lifetime of it, and all by the age of twenty-five. I knew I couldn't avoid loss, but I figured I could at least have some control over it; I could at least try to make it resemble gain.

Australia, Fiji, the Cook Islands, Holland, Italy, Spain, Norway, Japan, South Korea, Argentina, Uruguay: These are the names of my most recent gains and losses. I followed my instincts from one country to the next, finding a job, an apartment, building a life and then leaving it, losing it. Each country was a love affair, but a safe one; this time the object of my love was unlikely to reinvent itself overnight and more likely to give back.

In Australia I learned to surf. It turned out lying on my stomach on a board pressed to the heaving Pacific was the best thing for me. Riding wave after wave, learning the ocean's rhythms taught me all kinds of lessons about loss. After a day on the water, with a head full of sun and tight, salt-water skin, it was easy to feel that life was more about letting go than hanging on. There was some sense of pattern to my life, that, like surfing, if I could just manage to skate over the surface of things, I would not be dragged down.

Buenos Aires was a city living in the shadow of loss. Everywhere I looked in Buenos Aires, once-opulent buildings were crumbling. Everyone I talked to had a story about how they lost everything—property, businesses, jobs, and life savings—during the economic crisis of the late 90s. Overnight, the middle class became the lower class. And yet, everywhere there was music and dance. People were living life the way only those who have known loss can. Buenos Aires taught me that even loss can be beautiful, for there is nothing quite as beautiful as a city that has come through it.

Now, instead of being haunted by grief and loss on every corner, in every object, I am haunted by something much larger. I am haunted by how big and diverse I know the world to be. I'm haunted by the memory of dear friends living this very moment in faraway places and I'm comforted by the thought that I can always travel back to them. Instead of chasing Donovan through my dreams, I now chase places. In a recurring dream I am standing in a hot and dusty marketplace, looking at an ancient map. I decide I will take a boat down a river into the jungle and the man selling the maps tries to warn me. He shakes his head, lists the dangers one by one, but I always insist. In my dreams, I'm not afraid. I push forward, knowing there is no such thing as loss.

BUFFY CRAM'S SHORT FICTION and creative nonfiction have appeared in Canadian and American literary magazines and anthologies. In 2007, Buffy's memoir piece *Man Hands* won a National Magazine Award. In 2008 her short story *Loveseat* won third place in the Prairie Fire Short Fiction Awards. Since then her fiction has been short-listed or received honorable mentions in contests run by *Cutbank*, *Glimmer Train*, and the *Nimrod International Literary Journal*. After living in Vancouver, Montreal, Boston, South Korea, and Argentina, Buffy has decided to settle for a while in Austin. She is currently working on a novel.

Sandy Silver

Helping Others in Grief

WHAT TO SAY

THERE IS REALLY NOTHING to say to someone who has lost a loved one. We feel sad, helpless, and tongue-tied, but we feel better if we do verbalize our thoughts to them. At the time of my loss, the following words were said and worked for me:

- Mention the deceased person's name in what you say.
- I'm sorry.
- My thoughts are with you.
- I care about you and your family's loss.
- Mention an anecdote, happy memory, or story about the deceased.
- Mention something the deceased person said that is meaningful to you
- Mention the deceased person's virtues, achievements, or successes you remember
- The only time to say, "I know how you feel," is when the circumstances are the same.
- Avoid giving advice or simple explanations of the tragedy.
- Avoid dramatic language such as "dreadful" or "horrible."
- Avoid saying these things in a public place such as the grocery store, party, or church. Feelings are close to the top

and tears come easily. These tears are best shed as privately as possible.

- In the case of a self-inflicted death, avoid asking any questions. There are no answers.
- Avoid well meaning clichés like, "He is in a better place" or "Keep busy. You will get over it" or "Be grateful for what you have."
- In the loss of a child, avoid words like, "At least you have other children." A mother could have ninety other children, and the loss would still be devastating.

WHAT TO WRITE

IT IS DIFFICULT TO read the cards and letters immediately, but they are appreciated and will be savored in the future. The most important thing is to write in the first place. What you say is less important than the fact that you write.

- I'm sorry in a simple and direct way. Mention the name of the person who died. This is effective and comforting.
- Relate a happy memory about the deceased, some advice they gave you, the virtues or achievements for which they will be remembered. The more specific the story, the more meaning it has.
- If you are writing to a specific member of the family, be sure to include the other family members in your closing. All family members have their own ways of coping and mourning.
- Be specific in your offers to help. If you say you will call or do something specific, make a note to do exactly that at the time you said.
- Some people are uncomfortable with such blunt words as death, dead, died, killed, and even such milder euphemisms as passed on, passed away, departed, left this life, gone to a better life. Think of the recipient, and if they feel this way,

substitute "Sorry about your loss," or "Sad to hear about Chris."

- Indicate that your letter needs no acknowledgment or reply. Just be there for the person.
- Observe the fine line between sympathy and pity. Avoid making the person who has suffered the loss appear as a helpless victim of life's injustices. Read the letter aloud. Sympathy respects the person's ability to survive the loss while pity draws attention to the injustice and promotes martyrdom and defeat.
- Imagine yourself in the other person's place. Think what would work for you.
- Keep descriptions of your own feelings to a minimum.
- Keep it short.
- Make a note of the six-month mark. For most families, this is a difficult time as well as the birthday and holidays. Send a card saying that you still remember and you still care.

WHAT TO GIVE

THE FAMILY WANTS THEIR loved one to be remembered. Loss is sometimes swept aside and becomes the past when the present is greater for remembering the person and his or her contributions.

- Considering family preference and religious customs: flowers, donations to a charity, a Mass offering, or other type of appropriate memorial. Planting a tree is a welcome act of renewal.
- When sending flowers to a funeral home, address the accompanying small card's envelope to "The funeral of..." and enclose a brief message.
- A gathering place is needed for people to share the loss. It need not be the family's home. In the case of young people, it needs to be a place where they can talk with each other,

have their own music, and gain strength from sharing the mutual loss.

- Send a simple catered meal to the home. Ask the family when the best time would be. This can include many givers and can be for the future...perhaps holidays.
- Send a gift certificate for a massage or other treat.
- Give the "license" for the surviving family to be a little strange for a few weeks. Don't push. Accept what they are doing as something that works for them.
- Remember the survivors on holidays. (Example: One friend always remembers me on Christmas and Mother's Day with a card and note.)
- For some survivors, it works to remember the day the death occurred by calling or leaving a message. To mothers, it always seems like yesterday. For others, it is more difficult, and they are trying to forget the exact day. Your intuition will tell you what is appropriate.

There is plenty of time to plan permanent memorials such as trees or benches in favorite spots.

THINGS TO DO/JOBS TO GIVE

FRIENDS HAVE A NEED "to do something." It simply makes them feel better. It is difficult and overwhelming for the family to think about all these things. It is also difficult for some people to accept help. Just do it.

- Have a good friend answer the phone at the family's home. Have them identify themselves and be ready to give the caller a job when they say, "Is there anything I can do?" Keep a record of who called.
- Keep a record of who is doing what. Some jobs take several people. The job may not be hard, but the thinking about it is.
- Record the flowers and food that arrive at the home.
- Volunteer to do housework—sweep the porch, etc.

- Take care of the deceased person's room, clothes, etc. This does not have to be done immediately. Consult the family about the donation of personal things. Friends should move very cautiously through this. Families should not feel pressured to put away all of the deceased person's belongings.
- Write "Thank You" notes. This seems like an impossible task for the survivors because every stroke of the pen is painful. Groups such as a book club or bridge group can do this together with the survivors. Have the family decide on the proper note. Purchase the notes, order pizza, bring the envelopes and stamps, and do it as a group.
- Volunteer to pick up people at the airport.
- Volunteer to be the family spokesperson with the family's permission and instruction and work with the funeral home, church, etc. This is difficult for the immediate family.
- Help decide the appropriate charity. This may be a job for several people.
- Volunteer to write the obituary with the family's approval and work with the newspaper.
- Don't speak for the family unless you have been advised to do so. A friend of mine told me the following story after the loss of a child: "I had a special friend that I was waiting to see and she never came. I found out months later that she stopped at a neighbor's house to see how I was doing, and the neighbor advised her that I was too overwhelmed with people, food, etc. and that she should wait. I really wished I could have seen her at that time."

WHAT TO BRING

AS CHILDREN, SOME OF us were taught never to go to anyone's home without a gift for them—no matter how small. This seems to be even more important in the case of loss for both the giver and the receiver.

- Food ready to serve
- Flowers or a plant
- Big basket of candy
- Thank you notes, stamps, envelopes
- Bubble bath, aromatherapy, herbal teas
- Books
- Music
- Poems, letters, etc., written by the deceased
- One friend brought bread to the family every Friday for a year
- After a few weeks, give the family some of your favorite pictures of the deceased person with a note about happier times. Even years later, families appreciate photos and letters. This makes the deceased person's life grow when it has diminished. Don't ever think that it is "too late" to write or send things—such as a comment or a memory of a special event in the deceased person's life.

PLANS TO MAKE

MOST FAMILIES HAVE NOT thought of what is appropriate. Gather enough information to make their choice as easy as possible. When the family wants to do or plan a service that may be outside your traditional thinking or comfort zone, trust their judgment. A celebration of Chris's life held in a park was appropriate for my family and friends.

- Funeral service (private or public)
- Religious or church service (private or public)
- Burial, mausoleum, or cremation
- In the case of cremation, there could be a private or public service to spread the ashes
- Memorial in another city at a later time
- Some people—especially the elderly—like to help in the planning of their own funeral including the selection of the

funeral home, burial site, minister, favorite hymns, passages, and readings

- Know that any kind of music or service is appropriate as long as it is healing to the family. Music can include hard rock, heavy metal, or country and western music. Try not to censor the family's choices.

SANDY SILVER IS A mother of four, grandmother of six, author, teacher, and is in charge of making superhero capes in Spike Gillespie's Office of Good Deeds. She has lived in Austin, Texas since 1968 and is presently working as a personal assistant. Sandy has a B.S. from Indiana University and is a published author of two golf humor books, *A Man's Guide to the Justification of Golf* and *The Official Sandbagger's Guide.*

About the Editors

Photo by Ori

Spike Gillespie is a journalist, author, blogger, knitter, and wedding officiant in Austin, Texas. Her work has appeared in *The New York Times Magazine*, *The New York Times*, *National Geographic Traveler*, *GQ*, *Playboy*, and many other publications. Online her work has been published lots of places, too. Her blog resides at: *spikeg.com*. Her books include *All the Wrong Men and One Perfect Boy*; *Surrender: But Don't Give Yourself Away*; *Pissed Off: On Women and Anger*; and *Quilty as Charged*. She shares her life with her son, Henry; her partner, Ori; and four out-of-control dogs.

Katherine Tanney's novel, *Carousel of Progress*, was named Best First Novel by the Texas Institute of Letters in 2002. She has written several essays about love, loss, and living with dogs for "Modern Love" in the *New York Times*, and her nonfiction recently appeared in *Dirty Words: A Literary Encyclopedia of Sex*. She writes the column "Please Don't Feed The Writers" for the *Austin American-Statesman*, is a freelance journalist and blogger, and was featured in the book *Conversations With Texas Writers*. She also works in radio and is currently a part time announcer at Classical 89.5 KMFA.

For more information on the editors and contributors, or to connect with others stricken by grief, visit the **Stricken By Grief Network** at http://strickenbygrief.ning.com.